Pr...

By

On the Occasion of

Date

The *Quilt* of *Hope*

A Warm Patchwork of *Devotional* Thoughts

MARY TATEM

BARBOUR
PUBLISHING

All scripture quotations, unless otherwise noted, are taken from the King James Version of the Bible.

Scripture quotations marked NIV are taken from the HOLY BIBLE, NEW INTERNATIONAL VERSION®. NIV®. Copyright © 1973, 1978, 1984 by International Bible Society. Used by permission of Zondervan. All rights reserved.

Scripture quotations marked NASB are taken from the New American Standard Bible, © 1960, 1962, 1963, 1968, 1971, 1972, 1973, 1975, 1977, 1995 by The Lockman Foundation. Used by permission.

Cover image © iStockphoto

The author is represented by literary agent Janet Kobobel Grant.

Published by Barbour Publishing, Inc., P.O. Box 719, Uhrichsville, Ohio 44683, www.barbourbooks.com

Our mission is to publish and distribute inspirational products offering exceptional value and biblical encouragement to the masses.

Member of the
Evangelical Christian
Publishers Association

Printed in the United States of America.

5 4 3 2 1

Dedication

*To my son, Matthew Tatem, his wife Lisa, and
their children, Kaitlyn, Nathan, and Thomas, who have
walked in hope and expectation "to see the goodness of
the LORD in the land of the living" (Psalm 27:13).
They demonstrate courage and faith in the face
of adversity and are wonderful examples of
depending on God's grace to bring victory.*

Acknowledgments

Thank you to all the people who generously shared their fascinating stories with me. A special thanks goes to Nancy Gloss, owner of Nancy's Calico Patch, and to Mary Frances Ballard, who supplied resources for my research.

A big thank-you goes to my son, Andrew, who gave his time and skill to critique this book, adding greatly to its readability. And I'm grateful for the prayer warriors who faithfully talk to God about my writing.

Welcome to the Warmth of Hope

Hope brings joy and peace to our daily lives. Our souls cry out for hope, especially when we're in the dark places of life. When we look to God as our source of hope, our spirits rise and our courage is strengthened. We can trust God with the fabric of our lives and watch Him build a beautiful patch-work, using both the dark and the bright happenings of our days.

The following stories show how God's love and power can piece together the varied experiences of our lives, arranging them into lovely patterns as beautiful as any handmade quilt. God's Word and His mercy blend together to warm hearts and carry us through good times and bad. When we see the character of God as demonstrated in these stories, our hope in His goodness will soar.

Feast on these stories of people who have experienced the hope God freely offers His children. Enjoy the encouragement offered by the scriptures containing the word *hope*.

It is my prayer that this small devotional volume will cause you to hope in God.

MARY TATEM

A Touch of Home

After I looked things over, I stood up and said to the nobles, the officials and the rest of the people, "Don't be afraid of them. Remember the Lord, who is great and awesome, and fight for your brothers, your sons and your daughters, your wives and your homes."
NEHEMIAH 4:14 NIV

Sitting on his bunk in a primitive barracks, in a land devastated for centuries by rival powers, Dean tore into a package from his girlfriend continents away.

Loud guffaws rolled down the line of bunks when the opened box revealed a handmade quilt of pieced stars in quiet colors.

"A quilt! Little boy ready for his nappy?" Carl yelled, in one of the milder verbal jabs. A barrage of jokes accompanied playful punches from the men. The soldiers comprised a well-trained unit, built on easy camaraderie and trust.

"Shucks, I thought it was another care package full of cookies." Carl leaned over to look closer at the carton.

"There's more," Dean said as he held up a smaller box. "It's Laura's homemade caramels."

Brett made a grab for the caramels. "I get them all because I didn't tease, right?"

Dean outmaneuvered him and tossed several handfuls around the room. "There's enough for everyone," he said. The quilt was forgotten in the flurry of caramel grabbing.

Later that night, screeching rockets whistled overhead and exploded near the camp, shaking the men out of their sleep. Such barrages were a frequent enemy tactic.

After a chorus of curses and exclamations, the men laid back in their beds, each soldier immersed in his own thoughts. They waited for their adrenaline to recede so sleep could return, forcing their minds to quiet to allow their bodies much-needed rest in preparation for the rigors of the upcoming day.

> **Scrap Basket**
> One driving motivation behind quilt making is the desire to remain in someone's memory.

Dean pulled Laura's quilt closer to his chin in the cold barracks. He thought he could just catch the scent of her favorite perfume and guessed the other men might have liked a quilt themselves. With memories of home, the warmth of family, and the delights of one very special girl, Dean finally drifted off to sleep.

God's Pattern

Friendships are a gift. Friends encourage us
when we are down. In the military, God uses
the friendships and trust forged by hours
of arduous training to help soldiers endure
deprivation and survive danger. Memories of
home, more peaceful times, and God's goodness
to us in the past provide a place of mental
refuge when a soldier—or anyone—needs
respite from the realities of the moment.

The Warmth of Hope

"You will be secure, because there is hope; you
will look about you and take your rest in safety."

JOB 11:18 NIV

Engraved

Behold, I have graven thee upon the palms of my hands;
thy walls are continually before me.
ISAIAH 49:16

"Happy birthday to me. . ." Cindy sang when the mailman brought a large package. "Grant forgot it, but Grandma remembered."

Back inside the house, Cindy shook a scolding finger at her husband's picture on the mantel before tearing off the package's wrapping. A handmade quilt spilled onto her lap.

"Thanks for a perfect twenty-first birthday present," Cindy whispered into the lonely solitude of her tiny home. She stretched the quilt out to enjoy the pattern of connected green and yellow rings. Wind howled across the Nevada landscape, rattling the windows as if to mock her joy. Grandma and her Indiana hometown seemed far away.

"Why, this is a Wedding Ring quilt," Cindy exclaimed. *Trouble is, Grant has changed since we came to this military outpost base,* she thought. The barrenness of her surroundings mirrored the barrenness of her relationship with Grant. Trying to get him to talk seemed as futile as chasing the tumbleweeds that blew across the land—and he was just as prickly as that strange thistle if she trapped him into conversation.

"Grandma, what would you do in this vast, lonely place?" Cindy shook her head. "I'm really going batty—talking to myself more every day." When she thought about her childhood visits to her grandmother's numerous homes, she knew what Grandma would do. "I'll plant a garden and make a fountain in the middle of it like Grandma always did when she moved."

Cindy made a list of the vegetables she remembered helping her grandma can from the produce of her garden. She decided that when Grant came home, she wouldn't berate him for overlooking her twenty-first birthday—she would ask him to drive her to the feed store to buy seed for a Nevada garden. If Grandma could relocate and establish a place of beauty wherever she went, Cindy could, too. Twenty-one was an age of independence; by determination, she could make her home into a place of peace and order.

Cindy ran her finger over the embroidered name and birth date in her quilt's center circle, remembering that Grandma liked to say God had engraved her name on His hand. If God cared enough to carry Cindy's name on His palm, He could certainly bring her to contentment even in the midst of loneliness and isolation.

God's Pattern
We often see the palms of our hands through the course of a day. God, who engraves us on His palms, is aware of us all the time. And His interest is no passing fancy—God cares about every circumstance in our lives.

The Warmth of Hope
My soul fainteth for thy salvation:
but I hope in thy word.

PSALM 119:81

Fabric for the Heart

O taste and see that the LORD is good.
PSALM 34:8

These new red fabrics are great—they won't fade the way old red dyes did." Randall spread sample swatches for Mrs. Tindal's examination on a worn pine table, but his gaze never left Dorothy by the fireplace. Dorothy tried to stitch quilt pieces together while her little brother tugged at her arm.

"Read to me," Willy begged his sister for the tenth time.

Mrs. Tindal smiled at Dorothy. "Come over here and help me decide which calico will make the most serviceable dress for you this spring," she said. Mrs. Tindal moved aside to allow Dorothy to stand beside Randall.

Blushing, Dorothy selected a print of tiny red roses on a tan background. "Does this wash well?" she asked.

Randall couldn't look away from Dorothy's brown eyes long enough to see which fabric she held. He fumbled to take it from her and grabbed her hand instead. They stood still, red creeping up their faces.

"The other man who stops to sell cloth leaves Dorothy samples for her quilts," Willy piped up. "Then Ma can make her mind up later, and we can read while it's daylight." He squeezed his five-year-old body between Dorothy and Randall.

"Oh yes, of course." Randall tried to recover his salesman's air. Pulling a variety of swatches from his leather case, he said, "Perhaps these chintzes would complement your complexion."

Randall stopped cold. He'd almost said "peaches and cream complexion." Turning back to the table, he tried to recover his composure. "Or maybe you fancy gingham," he said, as he piled more swatches on the table.

"With all these pretty fabrics, it's hard to decide." Mrs. Tindal tried to put Randall at ease even as she suppressed a grin at the smitten couple.

"I'll leave the swatches," Randall said. "You can order when I return. Meantime, maybe Dorothy could use the samples in her quilting. The gold tones in these chintzes would set off the blues in your quilt stars." He motioned toward the quilt square Dorothy still held.

"If you leave so many, what will you show the

neighboring farms?" Mrs. Tindal asked.

"Oh, I've plenty more in my wagon," Randall answered, still gazing at Dorothy. "Use the samples. They'll prove how easy it is to work with our material."

"Thank you very much," Dorothy said, lowering her eyelids while her heart did a glad skip. "The golds will be lovely in my quilt."

God's Pattern

God gives us many opportunities to sample
His goodness. He wants us to "taste and see"
how good He is to us. Like the variety
the fabric salesman offered, God's
goodness takes many forms.

The Warmth of Hope

The hope of the righteous shall be gladness.
PROVERBS 10:28

Lifesaving Work

*D*onna tried to paste a smile on her face, took a deep breath, and opened the door. Then she trudged into the quilt store to begin her new job.

The store's owner, Ellen, turned and opened her arms for a hug. "I'm so glad you can work here," she said. "We really need your quilting experience. We're swamped with work."

"Good—busy days will help me not to think too much," Donna replied.

"You're right. While you're here, I hope you can forget about your divorce and the scary things your husband's doing." Ellen handed Donna a bright apron. "Working here will be a wonderful distraction. Quilters are the nicest people."

By noon, Donna was in complete agreement with Ellen's assessment. The cheerful customers chatting enthusiastically about quilt designs brought genuine smiles to Donna's face.

"Do you think this color will blend with my other

quilt fabric?" A customer spread a yellow smiley face print over a selection of other prints in her pile. "I want to use it for the border of my grandson's quilt," she explained. "He's struggling with anger over his dad, who left the family. Maybe sleeping with smiley faces on his bed will help him start looking for the good in things."

Donna laughed. "If it does, I'll make myself a blanket of solid smileys. I can sympathize with your grandson. It's hard to control your anger when someone has hurt you."

Donna chuckled again as she cut the bright yellow smiles for the woman. She straightened her shoulders. This job was good for her.

She enjoyed hearing the varied reasons women gave for the quilt designs they chose. Giving out helpful tips made her feel useful. Listening to customers when they revealed their assorted heartaches helped her regain perspective about her own trials.

"I'll pray for you," Donna said often, handing purchases to troubled customers. Rediscovering her spiritual foundations, she took tiny steps toward trusting God with her future.

> **Scrap Basket**
> In the mid-1940s, Dr. William Rush Dunton, Jr., a Maryland psychiatrist, decided the process of creating a quilt benefited his "nervous" patients. He encouraged the hobby, because he observed that working with other people on a creative project was good for mental health.

God's Pattern

Helping others always carries the benefit of improving our own outlook on our problems. Compassion is therapeutic.

The Warmth of Hope

Therefore my heart is glad, and my glory rejoiceth: my flesh also shall rest in hope.

PSALM 16:9

Remembering

*From the rising of the sun unto the going down of the
same the LORD's name is to be praised.*
PSALM 113:3

 $\mathcal{I}$ don't want to go." Jim rubbed his forehead.
"Memories of Dad's time in that hospital are painful.
A good hospital, but Dad died anyway. I don't think
some *memory quilt* is going to make me feel better."

"It's called the Remembrance Art Quilt. Don't
you want to see how my embroidered scripture and
your father's navy emblem fit in?" Janice put on her
earrings.

"Not really." Jim reached for the newspaper.

"Harry Lumpkin wants you there. You always
enjoyed talking with him when he was visiting his
brother and you were seeing Dad."

Jim put the paper down. "Is this some weird service, trying to please every religion?"

"I don't think so. First, the volunteer will unveil
the quilt, and then someone will read a sentence
telling a little about each person who died this year.
Harry wants you to be there to hear what he wrote."

Reluctantly, Jim put on his jacket. Later, at the

hospital, he examined the quilt closely.

Soon Harry Lumpkin was at Jim's side. "I'm glad to see this quilt," Harry said. "It helps me remember all the good things about my brother's hospital visit— how much the nurses cared and how hard the doctors worked to rescue him. See that word 'majestic' written at the top of the quilt?" Harry pointed. "Life is a majestic gift from God."

Jim looked up, where Janice's embroidery proclaimed, "In the rising of the sun and its going down, we remember."

His throat tightened as Jim thought of all the living this quilt represented. "Dad, I'll always remember," Jim whispered. He looked more closely at the cloth mementos that symbolized people's lives, the daily rising and going down. A baseball swatch, a family picture transferred to cloth, teddy bear material, roses embroidered here and there. Each stitched piece was a symbol of ordinary activity.

> *Scrap Basket*
> Quilts provide a way to hold on to treasured memories of our loved ones.

"I'm glad we came," Jim said in a husky voice, as he put his arm around his wife. "I've been reliving the pain of Dad's death too much. This makes me remember how much he loved living, how brave he was to get up every morning and go to work—even though his job was a bore and his boss a bear. It isn't the fabulous, dramatic events of living that matter in the long run. True nobility comes from loving God in the face of whatever the world throws in your face."

God's Pattern
Small things can be powerful reminders of the victorious lives of our departed loved ones. God, who knows the end before the beginning, is pleased with our daily acts of obedience and devotion—no matter how small or trivial they may seem to us. God highly values our trust in Him.

The Warmth of Hope
Let thy mercy, O LORD, be upon us, according as we hope in thee.

PSALM 33:22

Mystery Quilt

And he said unto them, Unto you it is given to know the mystery of the kingdom of God: but unto them that are without, all these things are done in parables.
MARK 4:11

"My stress just disappears when I come to the Mystery Quilt weekend," Jill said, turning the car full of quilters into the parking lot of a bed-and-breakfast. "Ready for some fun?"

"Sure am," Wendy replied. "Did everyone cut their fabrics into the sizes and shapes the directions gave?"

Trish held up a box. "Absolutely. But I'm puzzled about what we'll be piecing from them."

"That's the idea," Grace chimed in as the women stepped out of their car. "A mystifying mystery. The brochure says we'll only get one clue at a time." She twisted her long hair between her fingers. "I'm scared I won't be able to figure any of them out."

"I'm scared my choice of material won't blend well when we sew everything together and finally see the design we're making. The suspense is killing me." Trish tugged her suitcase out of the trunk. "I've never pieced anything bigger than a pillow before."

Jill handed each woman her own portable sewing machine. "I'm afraid I'll get carried away getting to know the other mystery quilters and go home with nothing done. I'd never hear the end of it from my family."

After a quick trip to the bedroom they would share, the women lugged their sewing machines into a roomy parlor.

> **Scrap Basket**
> The ready availability of books and patterns has reduced the mystery of making quilts—and made the hobby easier.

A delicious Lancaster dinner preceded the opening of the first clue. The whir of sewing machines didn't begin to compete with the babble of women getting acquainted and sharing their excitement over the weekend's activity. Jill's machine soon fell silent as she discovered the woman next to her had traveled all the way from England.

"Don't peek!" Gail, the hostess, frowned when Wendy started to turn her work to the right side after finishing the first seams. "No fair looking at the right side until you finish all the clues for the first square."

Trish groaned. "I can't stand the suspense."

"I'll never get it right." Grace twisted her hair.

God's Pattern

God enjoys sharing mysteries with us. If we pray and study His Word for direction, our understanding of His ways will grow. God rarely reveals everything at once lest we be overwhelmed. Instead, the Bible gives us clues that cause our understanding to slowly unfold—and God reveals Himself and His plans for us a little at a time.

The Warmth of Hope

For I hope in You, O LORD;
You will answer, O Lord my God.

PSALM 38:15 NASB

Push the Envelope

*Ah Lord God! behold, thou hast made the heaven
and the earth by thy great power and stretched out arm,
and there is nothing too hard for thee.*

JEREMIAH 32:17

The plane had barely taken off when the woman seated next to Dianna took out a pair of wooden knitting needles and began to click away.

"What are you making?" Dianna asked her seatmate as the airline television screens began showing safety information for the flight to Europe.

"I'm knitting a square for an afghan. My colleagues will make it into a quilt for a raffle. We hope to raise a lot of money where I work." The woman reached for her purse. "I have lots of raffle tickets right here—would you like to buy a dozen or so?"

"Uh," Dianna sputtered, stalling. "What kind of work do you do?"

"I manage a pediatric bone marrow transplant unit in a university hospital."

Dianna's eyes widened as she took in the brown corduroy overalls and bright tie-dyed T-shirt her seatmate wore. "Are you a doctor?"

"Dr. K." Friendly eyes crinkled to match her smile as she reached out to shake hands.

"You really do the knitting yourself?" Dianna's voice rose in surprise.

"Lots of nurses, even doctors contribute squares. We connect the squares and back the whole thing with bright, colorful fabric. We tie the layers together at each corner of every square. It makes a great prize for our raffle. We sell lots of tickets. The money helps the families of our patients who are in this difficult program."

> **Scrap Basket**
> Computerized sewing machines have revolutionized quilting. Speed and complex designs are attainable for anyone with a good modern machine.

Dianna pointed to the balloons knit into the square. "Why do you take the time to knit such a complicated pattern?"

"I like a challenge," Dr. K. replied simply.

"Running a bone marrow transplant unit sounds like plenty of challenge to me."

"Yes, I like to push the envelope. Many times a child comes to us when everyone else has given up hope, but we're willing to try. I love those brave kids."

"I'm surprised you work on the quilt yourself," Dianna persisted.

"I like the process more than the product," the woman answered. "Knitting keeps my hands busy on long flights and frees me to think about different ways to handle the dangerous and complicated process of a bone marrow transplant. I guess I really like facing the challenges of my work."

God's Pattern
Dedicated doctors worldwide have "pushed the envelope" of medicine to make many medical procedures safer. But as medical knowledge advances, we realize how much there is yet to learn—knowledge that only God possesses. Humans comprehend only a portion of God's knowledge. He is the One who gives insight to researchers, doctors, and nurses—and to all the rest of us.

The Warmth of Hope
Let Israel hope in the LORD:
for with the LORD there is mercy,
and with him is plenteous redemption.
PSALM 130:7

Slip and Slide

My heart is fixed, O God, my heart is fixed:
I will sing and give praise.
PSALM 57:7

"I'm glad I got here before you closed." Lisa was breathless after her dash from the parking lot into the store. "Do you still have some pink Minke material? I hope so." Lisa didn't pause for an answer. "You'll never guess what I did!"

Rachel greeted her most frequent customer and pulled the bolt of soft fabric from the shelf behind her. "What now?"

"I sliced an eight-inch gash in the backing of my quilt with my rotary cutter."

Rachel clapped a hand to her mouth. "How did you do that?"

"The Minke material is lovely because it's so soft—but that makes it slip and slide and wiggle around instead of holding still when you work on it. I used it as the backing for my sister's baby quilt, sewing around three sides, like an envelope. When I trimmed the seams, the Minke slid over, and I made a good long gash in it with my cutter. I'm glad it was only the backing and not the quilt top I'd spent so long piecing."

Lisa continued. "I wanted to dash over here for more material, but my boyfriend called. We had a big fight about going to church after we're married. We argued so long that I thought you might close before I got here."

Rachel cut the replacement fabric. "Maybe you should pin the quilt down before you trim the seams. Go slow this time." Putting the material in a sack, she added, "Maybe you should go slow about committing to your boyfriend, too. If he doesn't like church now, it won't get better after you're married."

"I know," Lisa admitted. "I've been in the Bible enough to know I should 'keep my heart fixed on God.'" Her eyes met Rachel's. "Maybe that means my boyfriend isn't such a good match after all. . . ." Lisa's voice faded.

> **Scrap Basket**
> For years, women rinsed fabric in vinegar to set the dyes and prevent the colors from running.

Rachel patted her hand.

"You're right," Lisa said quietly. "We don't love God the same way." As she picked up her package, she squeezed Rachel's hand. "I'm glad I got here in time to replace my material—and I'm glad you got me thinking about my commitment to God. I don't want to slip and slide around with Him."

God's Pattern

When we focus our hearts on God,
the foundation of our decisions and plans
is pleasing Him. Compromising leads us
away from commitment to God's ways.
A fixed heart doesn't waver.

The Warmth of Hope

The LORD taketh pleasure in them that fear
him, in those that hope in his mercy.

PSALM 147:11

Yucky Medicine

A merry heart doeth good like a medicine:
but a broken spirit drieth the bones.
PROVERBS 17:22

Y uck! That green stuff tastes awful." Barb twisted away from the spoonful of liquid her mother held out. "It makes me sick." She covered her mouth and nose with her quilt of blue and white squares. Even the smell of the medicine made her gag.

Worry lines formed on her mother's brow. "I know," Mom responded, "but this medicine is important to getting well."

If *she gets well*, Dad thought, as he stood in the doorway of Barb's bedroom. "What you need is incentive," he said to his daughter. "Look through this Sears and Roebuck catalog today while I'm at work. See if you can find something you'd like." Dad laid the thick book on Barb's quilt. "Find something worth lots of doses of yucky green medicine."

Wrapped in the cozy warmth of the simple quilt her grandmother had made for her, Barb spent hours perusing the catalog.

Dad returned home that evening, carrying a

Mason jar with a slit cut through its metal lid and a single nickel inside. He shook it in front of Barb. "What did you decide on as a reward from the catalog?"

Barb smiled. She had used a piece of yarn, undone from the ties in her quilt, to mark the exact page. "Look, Dad." She pointed to a fluffy organdy dress in the soft yellow color of a downy newborn chick. "Don't you think that's the most beautiful dress you've ever seen?"

Dad grinned. "My, my! How elegant my girl will look in that gorgeous dress. Now here's the deal: Four times a day, you take the green medicine and keep it down, and four times a day, Mother and I'll give you a nickel to drop in this jar. When there's enough to pay for the dress, we'll order it."

> **Scrap Basket**
> Before 1810, thread was expensive because it was handmade from linen or silk. Consequently, women often used quilt designs requiring minimum stitching.

"Won't that take an awful lot of nickels?" Barb asked.

"And worth every one to get my little girl well." Dad hugged her, then put the jar on the bedside table, silently praying the medicine would cure his daughter. "Time for a nickel," he announced, and Mother poured out a spoonful of green medicine.

Barb swallowed the liquid and chased it down with a quick drink of water. Dad handed her a nickel, and she smiled as it clinked in the jar. Four times a day, Barb shuddered but swallowed her medicine, often pressing her quilt tight against her mouth to help her keep it down. Four times a day, she dropped a nickel in the jar.

As the summer closed, Barb's smile widened. Not only was the jar nearly full, but she was feeling much better.

God's Pattern
God loves us and desires to sweeten our lives
with joy and wholeness.

The Warmth of Hope
That they might set their hope in God,
and not forget the works of God,
but keep his commandments.

PSALM 78:7

Fix Mistakes

Likewise, I say unto you, there is joy in the presence of the angels of God over one sinner that repenteth.
LUKE 15:10

*A*unt Margie, these points don't come together at the center like yours do. They're way off. Does that matter?" Lynn held her star square out for inspection.

"Afraid so." Aunt Margie put on her glasses. "The center of your star quilt will buckle if the first row of pieces don't match up right. Now's the time to rip them apart and start again."

"Rip them apart?" Lynn groaned. "That takes too long."

"Not with a good seam ripper, although I call it an *unsewer*. Much more positive term than ripper." Aunt Margie patted Lynn's shoulder. "No point in fretting over something fixable. Save your grief for something you can't fix."

"Like my dumb mistakes before I knew Jesus."

Aunt Margie shot Lynn a sharp look. "That was a long time ago."

"Yeah, but I'm still paying the consequences. I still can't vote, because I was convicted of selling drugs. And I'm locked out of a lot of job opportunities." Lynn's eyes reflected her regret.

"Wasting emotion on regrets saps energy." Aunt Margie ran the sharp point along a seam, pulling out stitches.

"I just wish there was a seam ripper for the past," Lynn said.

"There is," Aunt Margie replied. "It's called repentance. It gets rid of sin, just like a seam ripper gets rid of bad stitches. All you have to do is tell Jesus you know you've sinned and you're truly sorry. He paid the price for your sin—those things you now regret—by dying on the cross for you. When you repent, the sins are ripped out. Keep thanking God for what He did and let the regrets go."

Scrap Basket

In early America, women used a "paddlin' " stick to beat wet, soapy quilts on a firm surface. Women used both hands to bring it down hard and drive the dirt out of the quilt.

God's Pattern

Once we receive God's forgiveness through faith in Jesus Christ, God wants us to become productive people in His kingdom, using what we learned to teach others. There's no use in wallowing in continued guilt.

The Warmth of Hope

Behold, the eye of the LORD is upon them that fear him, upon them that hope in his mercy.

PSALM 33:18

A Promising Prom

*I was. . .naked, and ye clothed me: I was sick, and ye
visited me: I was in prison, and ye came unto me.*
MATTHEW 25:35–36

*A*rlene leaned back against the sofa pillow. Her
needle lay on the quilt she sewed. "I've been working
on this quilt forever."

"With the doctor forcing you to spend most of
your sixteenth year out of school, making a quilt is a
productive way to pass the time," Mother answered.

Arlene looked at the clock. "School's out. Maybe
Brian will come."

"I'll put the quilt away." Mother reached for the
work in progress.

"No," Arlene said. "Brian likes to see how much
I've done."

When the young man arrived, he had a surprise
for Arlene. "Guess what?" Brian asked, holding his
hands behind his back.

"Not another frog." Arlene giggled.

"Better." With an exaggerated bow, Brian laid an
engraved invitation on Arlene's lap.

THE PROM, it read. Arlene's eyes opened wide.

Sitting across from her, Brian asked, "Will you go to the prom with me?"

"How can I?" Arlene bit her lip. "I'd never have enough energy to dance. I'd feel tired, and you'd feel cheated."

"I never feel cheated when I'm with you, Arlene. We can have lots of fun laughing. We don't need to dance."

Arlene hesitated. "I'd love to see everyone dressed up."

"It would be fun for you to dress up for a change," Mother said, returning to the room.

> ### Scrap Basket
> The early green dyes were unstable and often faded into tan colors after exposure to light. The color became popular for Baltimore Album quilts after the dyes became more stable.

"What would I wear? Shopping would exhaust me."

"No problem," Mother answered. "I'll make a dress for you. After all the wedding gowns I've made, I can make an elegant prom dress. What color do you want?"

"Green. Emerald green, like the blocks in my quilt."

Soon Arlene's mother was unleashing all her dressmaking skills, including intricate embroidery, for her daughter's special outfit.

Seated at a prom table, wearing her gown, Arlene felt like a queen holding court. Her eyes sparkled as friends came by to talk. Brian kept her supplied with refills of punch. By the time the band took a break, Arlene was exhausted.

"Ready to go?" Brian asked.

Arlene hesitated.

"Remember, I said we'd go as soon as you were tired. We'll finish the evening at your house. Emerald Queen, show me your quilt progress."

"Okay—thanks, Brian. I'm not sure I would survive this year without all the company and the quilt work. This evening gives me hope I'm getting stronger. I'll bet I'm back in school next fall for our senior year."

God's Pattern
We bring hope and encouragement when we visit the sick, the discouraged, and those who feel imprisoned by life's circumstances.

The Warmth of Hope
For surely there is an end; and thine expectation shall not be cut off.

PROVERBS 23:18

The Grand Prize

*Jesus said unto him, If thou canst believe,
all things are possible to him that believeth.*
MARK 9:23

$\mathcal{S}$orry—I didn't have time to be very creative," Pam apologized as she added her project to the hand-crafted items already donated for door prizes.

"Someone will be tickled to win it," Millie said, motioning Pam to the nearest table.

There, the table hostess suggested, "Each one tell us something about yourself." The woman next to Pam twisted her napkin before introducing herself as Dora. With her eyes down, she named her children and their ages, then blurted, "I might as well tell the truth. My husband took off and married another woman. I don't know why I said I'd come today. I'm not good company. My feelings are suffocating."

"You came to the right place," the hostess responded. The ladies shared their conviction that God could change any situation. And they clapped when Dora's number was called for a door prize—Pam's quilt.

"I'm sorry my quilt isn't pieced like the others," Pam apologized.

"This is the perfect prize for me," Dora answered. "This Tree of Life picture—full of new branches—full of new life," she stammered. "This quilt's proof that God heard my cries. He'll give me a new life." Dora's face beamed.

Pam just stared. She hadn't read any meaning into the preprinted fabric picture. She had selected the material because the design looked like it would be easy to ma-

> ### Scrap Basket
> Preprinted fabric panels, which look like pieced quilts, come and go in popularity with busy women and beginning quilters.

chine stitch, thereby fulfilling her promise to donate something handmade. Well, somewhat handmade.

"Today my life's going to change," Dora declared. The ladies murmured their assent and commented on Dora's happy face.

A year later, Dora returned to the ladies' luncheon. Until she introduced herself, Pam didn't recognize her. A new hairdo and a radiant smile transformed her appearance. As the women enjoyed their meal, they observed Dora's transformed personality, also.

"You've kept us laughing so much, my stomach hurts," Pam said.

"Thanks to you," Dora replied. "You know the Tree of Life quilt hanging I won last year? I put it in my kitchen to remind me that God was changing my life. Even my kids hardly know me now. I thought I'd slog through life enduring whatever came, but God did an overhaul. And He didn't stop with polishing the chassis," she said, circling her much-thinner waist with her hands. "He changed the transmission. I'm running on all cylinders now."

"All that from a ready-made fabric panel?" Pam asked, shaking her head. "Who would believe so much could start from something so simple?"

God's Pattern
There is no limit to what God can do with a surrendered life. His intervention can exceed our hopes when we trust in Him.

The Warmth of Hope
Blessed is the man that trusteth in the LORD, and whose hope the LORD is.

JEREMIAH 17:7

Pioneer Week

*Thou lovest righteousness, and hatest wickedness:
therefore God, thy God, hath anointed thee
with the oil of gladness above thy fellows.*
Psalm 45:7

Joshua walked to the front of the fifth-grade classroom, hitching up his pretend holster. He repositioned his cowboy hat and brushed his flannel shirt, scattering the corn bread remnants of the class's pioneer lunch. Then he held up his quilt square. "I made my patch for our pioneer quilt out of Mr. Long's flannel shirt."

"It's dirty." Anne loosened the ribbons of her pretend sunbonnet and let it hang down her back.

" 'Course it is." Joshua frowned at Anne. "You can't be a good lawn mower repairman and keep your clothes clean like a prissy girl."

"Go on with your story about what your quilt square represents." The teacher, Mrs. Band, gave Anne a stern look.

"Mr. Long fixed our lawn mower every year, and he let me help. This oil comes from lubricating the machine so it will run smooth and quiet all summer. One of the books Mrs. Band assigned said that sometimes pioneer people made quilts in memory of someone special. I decided to use Mr. Long's shirt for my quilt square because he was a special friend to our family."

Joshua looked at the floor, then continued. "I remember how every time one of our pets died, he read verses out of the Bible to make us feel better. He read verses when we were happy, too. He said God gave us the 'oil of gladness,' so I cut out an oily part of his shirt to remember how God likes to see us glad." Joshua gave Anne a defiant look.

> **Scrap Basket**
> In pioneer days, women gave their rough wool a gloss by rubbing it with a smooth stone.

"I didn't feel glad when Mr. Long died this spring. But this square helps me remember the verses he read and feel better." Joshua's voice lowered. "That's why I used Mr. Long's stained shirt for the class pioneer quilt. I miss him." Joshua stopped, unable to say more.

Mrs. Band didn't ask him to continue. She handed his square to a woman sitting at a sewing machine in the back of the classroom. She promptly sewed the discolored patch to Anne's square.

God's Pattern

In the Bible, oil often represents the Holy Spirit. When we allow the Holy Spirit to guide our choices and we uphold the biblical standards of God, the "oil of gladness" comforts us and brings us joy and peace. Gladness permeates our lives when we study and apply God's Word.

The Warmth of Hope

For whatsoever things were written aforetime were written for our learning, that we through patience and comfort of the scriptures might have hope.

ROMANS 15:4

Hero Quilts

Thou therefore endure hardness,
as a good soldier of Jesus Christ.
2 TIMOTHY 2:3

I'm going to make you a quilt with dinosaurs on it." Will's nurse, Patty, held his head as he retched with dry heaves, the tenth time before noon.

Will flopped back on his pillow, too exhausted to react to his nurse's attempt to comfort. The chemo treatments he had received in preparation for his bone marrow transplant had devastated his entire digestive system. Moments later, he hauled his intravenous pole into the bathroom again.

In spite of Will's lethargy from drugs and sickness, Patty was rewarded with a glimmer of interest in his eyes when she later arrived with a quilt made from bright green dinosaur squares, alternating with plain lavender patches.

"I remembered you like dinosaurs." She hung the quilt, tied a permanent marker to a ribbon, and wrote on one of the empty squares: "Will, you are a brave warrior. You endure the treatments with courage and patience."

In the following weeks, even though Will's body reacted to the transplant with fever and rashes, he invited every doctor and nurse to sign his quilt as soon as they came into his room. They wrote about admirable qualities they observed in him, inspiring Will to muster more courage and keep his focus on the goal of good health.

"Good idea," Bob told Patty, patting the quilt. Since Will had no parents, Bob, one of the hospital volunteers, had offered to stay with Will all the time. "Because Will wants all the parents up here to sign it, as well as the medical staff, he's motivated to get up and walk the halls for exercise."

"I think I'll make one for all the patients when they check in on the bone marrow transplant unit. An autographed quilt will give them something positive to remember after they go home."

"Especially good for Will." Bob nodded. "With no family, the praise on the quilt helps him battle for his health."

Bob waved away Patty's thanks for staying with Will. "You get more than you give when you help someone. The bond between Will and me will last the rest of our lives. I love him like a parent would. When you see the way he endures pain and sickness, you have to call him a hero."

"All the kids on this unit are heroes," Patty said. "I want them to see their quilts years from now and realize others saw great qualities in them. Their lives are truly worthwhile."

God's Pattern
We become stronger people as a result of difficult trials or severe troubles. Turning to God for help, asking Him to stay in control of our lives, and keeping a grateful heart in spite of our circumstances build strength and prevents bitterness.

The Warmth of Hope
Uphold me according unto thy word, that I may live: and let me not be ashamed of my hope.
PSALM 119:116

Saved Tees

*And all thy children shall be taught of the LORD;
and great shall be the peace of thy children.*
ISAIAH 54:13

Look, here's Missy's soccer champion shirt." Carol held up a blue and gold T-shirt and moaned. "I don't think I can bear to cut it."

"Missy will enjoy it a lot more in this T-shirt quilt than she will as an outgrown rag stuffed in a plastic bag." Debbie applied spray starch to the edges of the freshly cut camp logo from another of Missy's childhood shirts.

"She was so proud when her soccer team won. We cheered ourselves hoarse at that tournament." Carol's eyes misted over.

"Cut it." Debbie handed her the rotary cutter.

"What if I haven't taught her all she needs to know when she goes off to college?" Carol cut a neat square around the team's name.

"You haven't," Debbie declared. She ironed freezer paper to the edges to help prevent the seams from curling. "It's impossible to anticipate every little thing that will test our children when they're on their own. We teach God's principles, then we pray the kids can apply them as their lives unfold."

"I'm just not ready for her to leave home." Carol wiped her eyes on the discarded back of the championship shirt. "I can't believe she's graduating from high school already. Maybe I should buy her a bunch of Christian books about dating for a graduation present."

"Carol, you're making the perfect present. A quilt with all her treasured T-shirt logos will be a great conversation starter in a new dorm, while she's meeting new friends."

"Oh, here's her Barney shirt. She was so cute dressed in it and dancing to Barney songs in front of the TV." Tears rolled again. "What if she falls in with the wrong crowd?"

"We'll pray as we sew these patches together and the borders in between. The final goal of raising a child is to let her go into the loving hands of God to become a profitable member of His kingdom."

"That's the scary part. What if she walks away from God?" Carol dropped her cutter to hug Debbie. "I'm glad you're here helping me. Not only do I need help making a quilt, I need your encouragement to let go of Missy. She has to follow God on her own."

God's Pattern

The progressive process of letting go of our
children as they grow up requires us to pray
as the years unfold. Instilling in our children a
love for God and a desire to follow His ways
prepares both our children and our own hearts
for the future, enabling us to trust God to make
up for any parenting failures.

The Warmth of Hope

The LORD is my portion, saith my soul;
therefore will I hope in him.

LAMENTATIONS 3:24

Wedding Blocks

And he saith unto me, Write, Blessed are they which are called unto the marriage supper of the Lamb. And he saith unto me, These are the true sayings of God.

REVELATION 19:9

"I hope Brad's sister doesn't pout the whole wedding long." Brittany tucked a plain muslin square into a wedding invitation envelope.

"Overlook it if she does." Brittany's mom finished cutting strips of yellow floral fabric. She planned to collect the muslin blocks at the wedding, then use the yellow fabric as the sashes between them in a quilt. "You did the right thing, asking her to be a junior bridesmaid. You keep on showing her love and spending time with her, and Kelly will eventually decide having you for a sister-in-law is better than having Brad all to herself."

"I hope you're right. Can you believe what she said at the bridal shower last week?" Brittany almost sputtered. "The very idea, saying Brad could marry a prettier girl!"

"Hon, she's only twelve. Big brother leaving home will bring a big change in her life."

"Maybe she would feel important if I ask her to hold the basket to collect the squares when the guests arrive." She paused, looking from the basket to the stack of muslin in front of her. "Do you think people will really write on the squares and remember to bring them to the wedding?" Brittany continued to tuck the blocks and the instructions for writing and signing it into the invitations.

"I hope so. Your guests will think it's an honor to be invited to the wedding, and they will want to add their name to the wedding quilt. Is this fancy enough?" Mrs. Bayer held up a basket with some of the border material woven evenly through the cane strips. "If Kelly holds it, the decoration will match her junior bridesmaid dress."

> ### Scrap Basket
> Signature quilts were used in the latter half of the nineteenth century to raise money for charity. Charging per signature and raffling the quilts raised money for temperance issues and women's suffrage.

"Beautiful, Mom. I'm glad you thought of this quilt idea. I hope the ones who can't come to the wedding will sign and mail the blocks back. I hope they'll be glad to be involved in our wedding, even if it's from a distance. A quilt from all these squares will make a wonderful keepsake. Maybe I'll make a miniature quilt of classmate signatures for Kelly's birthday."

God's Pattern

The excitement of planning a wedding is small compared to the joy we will experience when we meet Jesus, the heavenly Bridegroom of the wedding of the Lamb in heaven. Nothing will compare to receiving that wedding invitation. The details we do in preparation for an earthly wedding remind us to prepare our hearts to see Jesus face-to-face at that heavenly feast.

The Warmth of Hope

And now these three remain: faith, hope and love. But the greatest of these is love.

1 CORINTHIANS 13:13 NIV

Doll Delight

*"In everything I did, I showed you that by this
kind of hard work we must help the weak,
remembering the words the Lord Jesus himself said:
'It is more blessed to give than to receive.'"*
ACTS 20:35 NIV

Ellie caught her breath when she and her sister,
Brooke, entered the armory with their mother. "I
didn't think we were getting Christmas presents this
year," Ellie whispered.

Her mother smiled. "We wouldn't without these
marines." Ellie and Brooke joined the other children
sitting on the floor around a tall Christmas tree, which
was blazing with colored lights and surrounded by an
enormous pile of brightly wrapped packages.

Representing her quilt guild, Dawn stood beside
the marine commander. The basket at her feet held
the guild's handmade doll quilts.

The band ensemble playing "Jingle Bells"
was nearly drowned out by the chorus of children
singing, their pitch wandering off in a cacophony
of discord. The children sang loud, out-of-tune
"fa-la-la-la-las" to "Deck the Halls."

Tall marines, resplendent in blue dress uniforms, marched in formation toward the tree. The awed children hushed to hear their names called. One by one the packages were distributed. Proper marine posture not withstanding, smiles ruled military faces. Each time a marine laid a doll in a little girl's arm, Dawn pulled a small quilt from her basket, tucking it around the doll.

Ellie tugged at the sharp crease in the marine's pants. "Thanks, mister. How'd you know I wanted a blue-eyed doll?" His jaw struggled to maintain a stern look, but instead, unaccustomed moisture collected in his eyes as Dawn wrapped a small quilt around Ellie's doll.

> **Scrap Basket**
> In the second half of the twentieth century, children in church youth groups and Sunshine Clubs pieced quilts and gave them to hospitals or missions.

The child cradled her baby, leaning over to plant a kiss on the plastic check and cover its feet with her new blue quilt. "Your blankie matches your eyes, pretty baby. I won't let you get cold."

Brooke held her doll out to Dawn. "I didn't hope I would get a doll *and* a blanket."

Her mother wiped her eyes and whispered to Dawn, "The quilts look homemade."

"They are. One for every doll."

"God bless you. My girls will spend hours cuddling their dolls in those pretty quilts."

God's Pattern

Giving brings a joy and gladness beyond
the gift's value, which confirms the scripture
telling us it is more blessed to give than to
receive. It's impossible to outgive God. His
multiplication of our gifts in the form of
gladness brings us joy beyond measure.

The Warmth of Hope

Happy is he that hath the God of Jacob for his
help, whose hope is in the LORD his God.

PSALM 146:5

Lost But Found

What man of you, having an hundred sheep,
if he lose one of them, doth not leave the ninety
and nine in the wilderness, and go after that
which is lost, until he find it?
LUKE 15:4

*T*he last time I worked on the quilt was at the retreat. Sewing during the discussion session helped distract me from the pain, especially the memories. When I think about Bill dying in spite of my prayers, I feel like God abandoned me."

"Call the center and ask if the quilt is there." Allie decided not to comment on Grace's theological statement.

Grace shook her head. "It's been a whole year since we were at Stoney Center. If they found a half-finished quilt, they've no doubt given it to charity or thrown it away by now."

Allie pushed the phone over. "Give them a call and find out for sure. Those fabric pictures of you and Bill represent important memories. Try to find it. Most people won't throw away pictures. And think about the fabric. You can't replace the pieces you cut from Bill's clothes."

"On top of Bill's death, I don't want to face the disappointment of another loss—my memory quilt."

"It will stay lost if you don't try. Let me call." Allie dialed and handed the phone to Grace. A minute later, Allie covered her ears at Grace's happy shout.

"You do? You kept it? I'll drive over to pick it up."

"I'll go with you." Allie grabbed her purse.

At the camp, Grace hugged the quilt. "I can't believe you kept it."

"We hated to toss out pictures and hoped someone would eventually claim it," the receptionist explained. "None of the group coordinators staying here remembered anyone quilting. We kept it, figuring someone wouldn't want to lose all that work and the pictures."

> **Scrap Basket**
> Part of the appeal of scrap quilting is making an attractive design from small pieces of discarded fabric otherwise useless.

"I transferred a lot of pain into that quilt." Grace smiled over the quilt, stroking the soft fabric. "Somehow the hurt feels lighter now. God kept my quilt here for me even when I was too depressed to look for it. I didn't trust Him to heal my pain."

God's Pattern

God sees all our hurt and grief. The parable
of going after the one lost sheep demonstrates
the depth of His concern for us. We can
trust Him to comfort us in our pain,
to restore our joy and hope.

The Warmth of Hope

And we desire that each one of you show the
same diligence so as to realize the full assurance
of hope until the end.

HEBREWS 6:11 NASB

Lily in the Valley

He healeth the broken in heart,
and bindeth up their wounds.
PSALM 147:3

"I don't think I will ever get over losing Lily." Mandy cuddled her baby's teddy bear. "How can I recover hope for anything?"

Jack held his wife. "It's been a long three months, and she tried so hard to live. God knows how much we all struggled, and He'll help."

Mandy sank into her husband's arms, as if to seek their warm comfort. "I do know He prepared me for the fact that she wouldn't live through the heart surgery. In my mind, I saw us with her butterfly balloon that we bought for her surgery. We cut the string. Sorta a symbol of letting her go." Mandy's tears rolled. "I still hoped and prayed she wouldn't die. We waited so long for this baby, and we aren't getting any younger. Why did she have so many problems?"

"I think it's better not to ask too many 'whys.'"

Mandy and Jack's grief settled into them like a numbing drug as they went through the preparations to bury their beloved daughter. They knew the ceremony would help, and they planned one final good-bye. Before the guests left the graveyard, Jack and Mandy cut the string holding the butterfly balloon and stood watching the balloon float into the sky. They stood until it was only a tiny dot. When they could see it no longer, Mandy said, "Lily's soul rose to heaven just like the balloon."

Somehow the act of cutting the balloon loose also began the process of cutting Mandy free from the crushing, paralyzing grief. She still ached for her lost baby, but a plan formed as the balloon disappeared.

> ### Scrap Basket
> In pioneer days on the difficult trail west, people who died were sometimes buried in a quilt because wood was scarce.

"I'm going to make a quilt to honor our beautiful baby."

She began the next day by going through her daughter's treasured belongings and clothes. As she clipped and stitched, each step of creating the quilt brought another layer of healing to Mandy's heart.

"I've never seen anyone survive grief as well as you," her best friend, Rhonda, told her later, as she dropped off some encouraging Bible promises.

"Working on Lily's quilt comforts me. Don't you love her picture in the center block?"

"I'll bring you some more of that soft lilac fabric.

It's the perfect color for the lilies you're appliquéing around the picture."

"Sit a minute and read the poems Jack wrote," Mandy invited. "God inspired them."

Mandy and Jack knew that the pain from losing Lily would never quite go away, but they knew it would get easier and that God would continue to help them. Then, a few months later, to the older couple's surprise, they discovered that another baby was on the way. Perfect in every way, they named her Hope. She was a living reminder that there is always hope with God.

God's Pattern
In spite of how things look to our
finite understanding, God is infinitely wise
and good. He will enable us to cope with
whatever is necessary when we lean
on Him for His strength.

The Warmth of Hope
In the hope of eternal life, which God, who
cannot lie, promised long ages ago. . .
TITUS 1:2 NASB

Battle Quilts

*Put on the whole armour of God, that ye may be able to
stand against the wiles of the devil.*
EPHESIANS 6:11

"Heavy and hot." Ted reluctantly thrust his arms
through the armholes of his ballistic-armor vest.

"Protective and preserving," Craig said, don-
ning his own. "Miserable as wearing armor is in this
oppressive heat, I'm glad for the protection of the
Kevlar sheet and ceramic plate in the middle of our
vests." Craig slapped his vest with his hand. "I read
that soldiers in days long ago only had heavy wool
batting to protect them. Can't imagine that protected
against much."

Ted overlapped his vest in front for double protection of his chest and fastened the Velcro strips to
hold it firm. Strong stitching held the layers in place,
much like the stitching on quilted vests of yester-
year. They fell silent as their thoughts centered on
what was about to happen. Hours of training focused
their minds on mentally rehearsing their plan and
squelched nagging thoughts about the vicious intent
of the terrorists to destroy them.

Only moments later, adrenaline surged through the two friends as their unit stormed a compound suspected of housing terrorists. Rifles ready, Craig and Ted took turns leading the rest of the squad as they burst into houses. Using the element of surprise to prevent the terriorists' escape, the soldiers moved forward rapidly. Only after returning to rest from the day's dangerous encounters did the disciplined men reflect on their mission's ultimate purpose: maintaining freedom in the world, especially in this barren corner of the world where men had not known the privilege of freedom. When he doffed his vest, Craig gave grateful thanks for its thick protection.

> ### Scrap Basket
> The first quilting of three layers of material was done for the protection of firemen and warriors. A thick middle layer of wool batting provided additional thickness, slowing a weapon before it could penetrate and pierce the body.

God's Pattern
Sometimes what seems like a hot, heavy burden is actually a provision from God that gives a protective covering for our lives. We put on the protection of God by training our thoughts to agree with His Word, requiring our actions to follow His ways, and obeying His guidance.

The Warmth of Hope

We wait in hope for the LORD;
he is our help and our shield.

PSALM 33:20 NIV

Treasure Hunt

*He will be the sure foundation for your times, a rich
store of salvation and wisdom and knowledge;
the fear of the LORD is the key to this treasure.*
ISAIAH 33:6 NIV

*Y*o-ho-ho!" Theresa greeted the vanload of ladies entering her store by slashing a plastic cutlass
through the air. "There's booty in the pirate chest."
She and her partner, Ann, tipped their pirate hats
toward the corner.

The six women selected free quilt-block kits
from the chest. "The colors match the kits we picked
up at the first seven stores," Ramona said.

Amber was just as excited. "Three more treasure-
hunt shops will complete the makings of a free
quilt."

"If my pocketbook and energy make it through
all eleven stores." Peggy sat down.

"I found the hidden treasure!" Ramona called,
waving a ruler. Each lady claimed her ruler and selected fabrics to purchase.

As they were still browsing in the store, Ramona's cell phone rang. She blushed as she answered it,

sending an apologetic smile to her friends. Then her voice dropped. "I'm so sorry about the argument," she whispered into the phone. "I want us to stay together. I'll be home today when we finish the treasure hunt; then we can talk. Too many people around now." Ramona hung up. Seeing sympathy in Theresa's eyes as she rang up Ramona's purchases, she sighed. "Any pirate treasure that can fix a tattered marriage?"

"Let's say a quick prayer." Theresa pulled Ramona behind a tall display and prayed for God's wisdom and help in Ramona's marriage.

"They sound like they'll come back to our store," Ann observed, watching the women walk to their van.

> ### Scrap Basket
> Mutual interest in quilting forges lasting friendships. These friendships provide motivation for many quilting activities.

"This treasure tour may help the store recover from our recent business slump." Theresa looked at the paper where Ramona had scribbled her phone number. "And maybe God will use us to help Ramona's marriage slump."

Theresa picked up her cutlass to welcome another carload of women on the quilt-shop treasure hunt. The lure of free trinkets and a chance to win one of three expensive prizes kept carloads of ladies excited about two days of driving along the Pennsylvania Turnpike.

"I think the best treasure our store offers all

year-round is sympathetic listeners and a chance to pray about problems," Theresa said as the last carload of the day drove off.

"No better treasure than hope in God," Ann agreed.

God's Pattern

The fear or awe of God is the starting point for understanding God. The knowledge of God provides wisdom for our day-to-day interactions with people. In emotionally difficult times, what we know of God and His character is a powerful source of strength. Neither riches nor excitement is the ultimate treasure for satisfying living. The greatest treasure in life is knowing God and enjoying a personal relationship with Him.

The Warmth of Hope

Know also that wisdom is sweet to your soul; if you find it, there is a future hope for you, and your hope will not be cut off.

PROVERBS 24:14 NIV

Quilting for Sanity

For God hath not given us the spirit of fear; but of
power, and of love, and of a sound mind.
2 TIMOTHY 1:7

I brought you something." Myrna peered into the
dark log cabin from the doorway. She spotted Bertha
rocking by the fireplace. Billy wailed in the cradle
near Bertha's feet.

Myrna scooped him up. "Billy's ready for lunch."
She placed the infant in the crook of Bertha's arm.
Billy's mother stared straight ahead and just rocked.
She's worse than I thought. The baby rooted around
the front of his mother's dress.

Myrna unbuttoned Bertha's bodice and helped
the infant find his nourishment. Bertha finally
looked at her child. "Don't do no good. They all die
out here. Iffen it isn't one thing, it's another. This for-
saken place kills us all."

"I'm so sorry you lost your younger sister. I know
you miss her company and help." Myrna glanced at
the rough-hewed table still cluttered with tin plates
and crocks from breakfast. "I brought you something
fun to do to take your mind off your troubles." She

knelt in front of Bertha's downcast face. "Look at these pretty fabrics." Myrna unwrapped her parcel. "The stagecoach brought samples from Papa's Baltimore dye factory. Mother enclosed a sample and pattern for a quilt block stylish in the East."

Bertha looked at the pink tulip appliquéd on muslin. "I wanted to plant tulips on Rosie's grave, but mice et the bulbs I brought west on the covered wagon." One hand stroked the fabric flower.

Encouraged, Myrna laid out some already-cut pink petals. "When Billy finishes nursing, you and I can start stitching pretty squares and have a good visit." Myrna piled dirty plates into a dishpan and poured water from a pitcher, setting them to soak. She covered the bread with a cloth, then pulled up a chair near Bertha.

> **Scrap Basket**
> Quilting allowed pioneer women to provide their homes with a splash of beauty. The creative process provided mental distraction from days filled with burdensome chores and dreary living conditions.

"Why'd you come? Don't no one come visit way out here."

"I remember how lonely and isolated I felt when we first homesteaded out here. During last week's dust storm, I thought about you, losing your sister and all. To get my mind on something pleasant, I quilted all day long. Amazing how stitching something pretty lifts one's spirits. Let's get started." Myrna lifted now-sleeping Billy and tucked him back in his bed. With relief, she saw Bertha pick up pink pieces and arrange them into a tulip.

God's Pattern
Remembering the power of God helps us keep a sound mind in circumstances that threaten our sanity. God can overcome our troubles. God's power frees us from the prison of unfruitful thinking and gives us hope.

The Warmth of Hope
Turn you to the strong hold, ye prisoners of hope: even to day do I declare that I will render double unto thee.

ZECHARIAH 9:12

Holes

When thou passest through the waters, I will be with thee; and through the rivers, they shall not overflow thee: when thou walkest through the fire, thou shalt not be burned; neither shall the flame kindle upon thee.

ISAIAH 43:2

Alice swallowed two large capsules with a glass of water, hoping the strong painkiller would hurry and relieve her misery. "Ow." She eased back down on the sofa and pulled her grandmother's quilt closer around her neck, as if it could somehow block out the pain from her abdominal surgery.

She propped up a book and lit a cigarette, hoping to lose herself in a novel until the medicine took effect. The medicine worked faster than she expected, and she fell asleep.

The smell of singed material awoke Alice. Groggy from her medicine, she struggled to sit up. "Ouch!" She fell back, her muscles protesting their surgical abuse. Her cigarette rolled to the floor. "No!" Alice forced herself to sit up despite the pain. She stared at a hole the size of a quarter in her grandmother's Starburst quilt and pulled the phone over.

"No, don't call the fire department," Alice told her housekeeper over the phone. "Nothing has caught on fire, Maizy. There isn't any smoke. I think the quilt smothered a fire and maybe saved my life. I was too dopey from the painkiller to wake up. How dumb to take a narcotic painkiller and smoke! Except for Grandma's quilt, I might have died." She examined the singed edges of the quarter-sized hole. "Grandma spent years putting six thousand itty-bitty pieces together for this quilt, and I ruined it."

Alice peered through the hole. "Maizy, would you like this quilt? I don't want it around to remind me of what a dunce I was."

Alice nodded as she listened to Maizy lecture on the other end of the phone. "You're right, of course. I shouldn't smoke at all. It isn't good for my health." After a pause, she said, "You're right again. Better to have a hole than to smother in a fire. Better to have the reminder of my grandmother's love than not at all."

Alice laid her head back wearily. "Yes, it's a good parallel. God does want us to repent of small mistakes and mend our ways before they become a big fire. Yes, of course, Jesus forgives. Now don't worry about me." Alice hung up the phone and pulled the quilt up again, grateful for the friendship of Maizy and the legacy left to her by her grandmother.

God's Pattern
When we believe Jesus died for our sins and repent of them, God forgives us. When we feel like life is burning us and circumstances will drown us, God is walking with us through the fiery trial, and we will emerge unburned.

The Warmth of Hope
Rejoicing in hope; patient in tribulation; continuing instant in prayer. . .

ROMANS 12:12

Dreams

I delight to do thy will, O my God: yea,
thy law is within my heart.
PSALM 40:8

$\mathcal{Y}$ou're quiet. What're you thinking about?"
Blanche asked her sister, as they worked on their
quilts under the live oak on their front lawn.

"Same thing you're thinking about." Greta giggled. "Who will I marry? Who will sleep under this
quilt with me?" Greta rested the quilt square on her
lap and looked out over the field to the next farm.

"Hmm. Are you dreaming of a tall, dark-haired
farmer's son who is apprenticed to the village black-
smith?" It was Blanche's turn to giggle. "He'll bring
black grime to bed under that pretty red, white, and
blue Ohio Star quilt."

"I dare say he'll bring more money home than
your blond hero driving a wagon up our lane as we
speak. Reuben will bring hay and the smell of manure home to your quilt."

Blanche stuck out her tongue at her sister, smoothed
her skirt, and pulled one long curl to lie gracefully over
her shoulder. She bent demurely over her handwork.

"Mighty pretty work you girls are doing." Reuben climbed from the wagon seat and draped the reins over the hitching post. "Blanche, after I deliver these cheeses to your pa, would you have time to walk to the creek? Mother wants to plant some day-lilies along the fence, so I thought I'd see if any were blooming." Reuben hoisted two large cheese wheels to his shoulders.

"I have time." Blanche gave Greta a look that dared her to mention the bread ready to be punched down. "Pa's in the barn."

"Straw will match the yellow in your quilt," Greta teased when Reuben was out of hearing range. "Do you think he brought the cheese as an excuse to talk to Pa about courting you?"

> **Scrap Basket**
> In the mid-1800s, women were encouraged to pursue patchwork as a way to use all their spare moments purposefully.

Blanche turned serious. "What if Reuben isn't the right man? What if I'm being silly about him because he's so handsome? I'm a little scared. Who does God want me to marry? What's His will for my life?" She fiddled with her sewing supplies in the basket. "Do you think Pa would approve of Reuben courting me?"

Greta dropped her teasing manner. "I think so. Reuben goes to church regularly. I was just teasing about the manure smell. God knows what is good for you."

God's Pattern

We are wise to talk to God about our hopes and dreams and ask Him to conform our will to His. The Bible directs us to marry someone who loves Jesus wholeheartedly to prevent an unbelieving spouse from diluting our love for God.

The Warmth of Hope

"We have been unfaithful to our God by marrying foreign women from the peoples around us. But in spite of this, there is still hope for Israel."

EZRA 10:2 NIV

Firebreak

And let the beauty of the LORD our God be upon us:
and establish thou the work of our hands upon us;
yea, the work of our hands establish thou it.
PSALM 90:17

Sarah, grab the quilts off the beds and soak them in the horse trough."

"What?" Sarah looked with confusion at her mother. "They won't dry before bedtime."

Corrine grabbed her daughter's hand and directed her attention to the western horizon. "Quickly! A prairie fire's coming our way. Betsy, ring the bell to call your brother in. He can help hang the quilts at the windows. They'll be heavy when they're wet. I'm going to hitch Old Sam to the plow," Corrine called over her shoulder as she ran to the barn.

Old Sam seemed skittish. "Come on, boy." She urged him forward, pulling the widest blade to plow a wide furrow around the house. She kept the horse moving until the furrow completely encircled the house, turning all the flammable grass and vegetation under.

After closing all the shutters, Luke and Sarah

struggled to nail the sopping-wet quilts to the insides of the windows.

"Do we have to nail holes in my birthday quilt?" Sarah protested.

"Better a holey quilt than a burned-down house." But Luke nailed through the backing instead of the front.

When they were done, he relieved his mother, who was making a third furrow around the house, turning up the moist soil. Anxiously, the family looked to the west.

> **Scrap Basket**
> Sometimes pioneers laid quilts over the covers of their wagons for extra protection from rain.

"It looks like it has shifted north and isn't coming closer. Let's plow around the barn in case the wind turns it this way again," Mother suggested.

"Will the house burn?"

"I hope not. We've worked hard to do our part; now it's time to pray and ask for the Lord to bless us and allow our work to keep us safe."

"Please, God, bring Paw home from town," Betsy prayed, carrying cages of squawking chickens into the house. As if in answer, a cloud of dust appeared on the horizon to the south.

"It's Paw!" Luke shouted, as the laboring horse galloped up.

"Good job!" Vance hugged his wife. Together, they stood and watched the smoke. Vance held a finger up to judge the wind direction. "It's blowing north.

The Lord heard our prayers. The fire will miss us."
The family gave thanks as they watched and prayed
for other settlers on the frontier.

God's Pattern

After prayer, we must apply ourselves to
our work with energy and diligence. The
combination of our work and our hope in God's
help accomplishes results more than our labor
could accomplish by itself.

The Warmth of Hope

He that ploweth should plow in hope;
and that he that thresheth in hope
should be partaker of his hope.

1 CORINTHIANS 9:10

Hope Rescued

That being justified by his grace, we should be made heirs according to the hope of eternal life.
TITUS 3:7

 I'm concerned about Scotty's reading." Marta poured iced tea into two glasses.

"Is he your student with the sick father?" her husband, Dan, asked.

"Yes. In spite of his dad's illness, you'd think Scotty would do better in our reading-improvement program. He's smart as a whip and very verbal. I'm worried, because he isn't reaching our goals. After twenty weeks of Reading Recovery, we hope the kids achieve the average class reading level."

Their son, Tommy, grabbed his mother's hand. "Can we bless the food before we psychoanalyze your students? I'm starved."

Marta was still pondering Scotty's reading problems later, as she and Dan cleared the table. "You'd think he'd be a good reader. Today, he acted as confused as if I were teaching him to read Egyptian hieroglyphs. He wears me out. When I try to teach him, I feel like I'm slashing through a jungle of tangled vines which block learning."

"The Reading Recovery program has rescued lots of kids," Dan encouraged. "I'll bet Scotty succeeds. If not this year, he'll reach grade-level reading by the third grade." Dan put away the leftovers.

The phone rang. After hanging up, Marta turned a stricken face to her husband. "Scotty's father died." Marta stared into space a few moments, then Dan walked over and hugged her. She leaned against him a moment, then broke away and began to pull fabric from a chest in the corner.

"What are you doing?" Dan asked.

"I'm going to make a quilt. I'll use these ocean fabrics, because both Scotty and his father loved the

> **Scrap Basket**
> The more acute the fabric angle, the harder it is to piece. Proper equipment helps ease difficult quilting tasks.

ocean. Their last trip together was an outing to the aquarium."

"I thought you were exhausted," Dan protested.

"I want to comfort Scotty."

After the funeral, Marta told Dan, "It was worth a couple of very late nights of sewing. Scotty's mother said Scotty calls my gift his 'memory quilt', and he sleeps with it."

God's Pattern

Several states offer Reading Recovery,
a program that identifies children with reading
problems and provides special help. Assisting
children with their reading skills improves
their learning, bringing hope for a brighter
future. Reading the Word of God teaches us
the way to eternal life and brings us hope.
When we are heirs of His grace, the
possibilities for our future are limitless.

The Warmth of Hope

The eyes of your understanding being
enlightened; that ye may know what is the hope
of his calling, and what the riches of the glory
of his inheritance in the saints.

EPHESIANS 1:18

Welcome Quilts

*Thou preparest a table before me in the presence
of mine enemies: thou anointest my head with oil;
my cup runneth over.*
PSALM 23:5

*T*odd moaned, his hand reaching toward the wound in his chest, where the surgeon had implanted a central line. "It hurts." The nurse gave the five-year-old more medicine, then wheeled him to his room in the hospital's bone marrow transplant unit. A big welcome kit lay on his bed, providing a wonderful distraction from his misery.

"Look at all the exciting presents we have for you, Todd. We've arranged a great big welcome kit to show you how glad we are to get to know you in our little world on the fifth floor. We hope to make your stay with us as positive as possible," Nurse Pristol said.

The wide, contagious smile Todd flashed at the nurse as she helped him get comfy in the bed snagged her heart, and she became his instant fan and biggest cheerleader.

Todd discovered one grand surprise after another

as he dug into the kit. "How did you know I liked dinosaurs?" Forgetting the pain in his chest, Todd set the plastic models on the hospital table that swung over his bed. Coloring books, stickers, crayons, and marking pencils spilled onto the bed. "My most favorite character." Todd spread out the new quilt featuring a bear in the center, a familiar brown one with a cute, round tummy. "How'd you know I like Winnie the Pooh?"

> **Scrap Basket**
> Many organizations make quilts for sick and injured children in hospitals. If you are interested, visit your local quilt shop.

"We have our ways." The nurse grinned. "We know a lot about you. We're acquainted with all kinds of information about your blood and your favorite things, but we had to meet you to know about your wonderful smile and the twinkle in your eyes."

Todd clutched his new Winnie the Pooh quilt. Burying his face in the soft fabric, a welcome drowsiness blanketed him, bringing relief from the surgical pain. He slept.

"What a trooper," Nurse Pristol whispered. In spite of surgery pain, Todd wore a broad smile in his sleep.

God's Pattern

Wonderful volunteers care about young patients they have never met, patients who face the grim ordeal of bone marrow transplant. They prepare quilts and a bounty of toys to greet the children and ease their way through the difficult and dangerous weeks of bone marrow transplant and recovery. Our loving God cares about our troubles as we face the struggles of life. The difference is, He knows all about us. He prepares a table of comfort, provisions, and delights even in the midst of our trials and heartaches. Knowing Him as our refuge and our hope enables us to smile even through problems.

The Warmth of Hope

Be not a terror unto me:
thou art my hope in the day of evil.

JEREMIAH 17:17

Butterfly Hope

But we all, with open face beholding as in a glass the glory of the Lord, are changed into the same image from glory to glory, even as by the Spirit of the Lord.
2 CORINTHIANS 3:18

"Fascinating, I didn't know butterflies change the atmosphere." Janet turned in her hospital bed to see her visitor better.

Cara elaborated. "They aren't like birds that fly from point A to point B. They meander around and fly in random patterns, creating bits of haphazard airflow. Their wandering flights make minor changes in the normal way weather is predicted. That's why I brought you the butterfly poster. Think about butterflies when you're feeling bad about the interruption your pulmonary embolism caused."

"I'm only thirty-five. What an unexpected development! I'm fortunate to be alive, but I hope collapsing in the middle of my fifth-grade environmental science class didn't traumatize my students. Dr. Welsh said only a small percentage of people with undetected pulmonary embolisms make it." Janet took Cara's hand. "Thanks for the poster. I'll think of butterflies changing the weather when I'm frustrated about why this had to happen."

"My quilt store carries lots of beautiful butterfly material. When you get home from the hospital, would you like to join a class and make a butterfly quilt?"

"Seems like a good way to stay busy and keep from worrying while I recover. Dr. Welsh said recovery takes time. I'll need a distraction."

By the time Janet finished her quilt, she had a new peace about what had happened to her and a fervent passion for her new hobby.

Scrap Basket
The Women's Christian Temperance Union made and raffled quilts to raise funds. Convinced that much of society's poverty and family neglect resulted from men's alcoholism, the organization used its money to call attention to the problem of alcoholism. Their goal was to change society for the better.

God's Pattern
God desires us to become Christlike, but on our own, we only change bit by bit. When we encounter unexpected events that challenge our routines or views, we know God can use even the difficult or unpleasant situations to make us more like Jesus. This knowledge gives us comfort and brings us hope. Our hope is planted in God's goodness. We trust Him to bring good out of the events of our lives.

The Warmth of Hope

Why are you downcast, O my soul? Why so
disturbed within me? Put your hope in God, for
I will yet praise him, my Savior and my God.

PSALM 42:5–6 NIV

Cat Business

*"The LORD your God is with you, he is mighty to save.
He will take great delight in you, he will quiet you with
his love, he will rejoice over you with singing."*
ZEPHANIAH 3:17 NIV

If I beg nicely, would you make one of these quilts for *my* cat?" Ami folded her hands as if in prayer and dropped to one knee in front of her friend.

"You silly!" Kendra laughed, swatting at her.

Ami grabbed her hand to pull herself up. "Seriously, these cat quilts are elegant enough to be sold as decorator items in fancy interior design stores."

"I'm thinking of doing just that. I was so discouraged when my health forced me to quit teaching. Now I have the embryo of my own cottage industry." Kendra stroked her cat, who was curled up on a two-foot-square quilt made from coordinating strips of tapestry-quality material.

"Do you want tassels and braided trim on your quilt?" Kendra asked.

"I want it all if it will keep Tabby on the quilt and off the upholstery."

Kendra chuckled. "I don't know why, but cats

seem to love the soft, yet textured, feel of my fabrics. They choose to sleep wherever the quilt lies in preference to sofa cushions. And, believe it or not, this fancy material washes like a dream."

"Look out, cat hair! No more shedding business suits. My friends will think I'm the cat's meow, pun intended, with a custom-designed quilt. I love the sophisticated colors and borders you use, a real work of art. Can you put a cat medallion in the middle?"

"Always do."

"I'll write a check." Ami opened her purse.

"No. You get my last gift; then I'm going commercial. Listen. Do you hear God singing? He's delighted because I found a new life when I couldn't teach. He's rejoicing over my new business."

"Kendra, when I'm with you, I always see the joy of the Lord. I grab some for myself just to remind me He cares about me, too."

God's Pattern

What joy to realize that God's will for us is
not something repugnant. Instead, it is the
fulfillment of desires He planted in our hearts
long ago. Those interests God cultivates in us
contribute perfectly to the tasks He designs for
us to perform. In His love, He directs us toward
those activities that fulfill His will. We discover
that fulfilling His will gives us great delight and
causes our hearts to rejoice. He brings quiet to
our hearts when we do what He calls us to do.
His song of delight resounds through our soul.

The Warmth of Hope

Guide me in your truth and teach me,
for you are God my Savior, and my
hope is in you all day long.

PSALM 25:5 NIV

Camp Feel Better

For he satisfieth the longing soul, and
filleth the hungry soul with goodness.
PSALM 107:9

*L*ook at my cool tree color!" Dillon held up the green fabric he had dyed. "We can cut out a whole forest of neat trees for Wesley's quilt."

"Mine looks like brick color, so we can cut out houses to represent Wesley's village." The boys were shaking out their fabric behind the summer camp craft tent, where a line hung between two trees in the woods. Scott hung his freshly dyed material to dry over the taut cord.

"Poor Wesley. He's been in the hospital, like forever," Dillon said.

"Yeah, twelve months. I'm glad I didn't have to stay that long. I was sick of hospitals by the time I could go home. And I thought *my* stay was long! No wonder the counselor said Wesley was homesick. I like her idea to make this year's quilt look like Wesley's village." Scott looked at his hands. "Yuck, red, like blood."

"Put my green hands with yours, and we look

like Christmas." The boys grabbed hands and began to wrestle.

"You win." Dillon rolled on the ground. "Man, I still get tired fast. I wish I was as strong as before I was sick."

"Laps in the camp pool help." Both boys sat on the ground, winded by their exertion. "Camp's a great payback for being in the hospital. Dad could never afford to send me to summer camp, but I'm having an awesome time here. Hope the quilt raffle makes money so I can come to next year's camp," Scott added.

> **Scrap Basket**
> German pioneers dyed cloth brown by using bark from the butternut tree. Hemlock and elder combined with alum mordant were used to make a reddish brown.

"Yeah, I hated being sick, but camp helps make up for it. Mom still gets nervous about me. She never would've let me come to a camp without special nurses like here."

"There's the gong." Scott stood up. "Race you to the dining hall." The boys took off, thoughts of illness sidetracked by times of fun.

God's Pattern

Adults go to great lengths to ease the suffering
of sick children. In addition to their physical
bodies' healing, we work to help children
develop healthy emotions that aren't warped by
their unpleasant experiences. God is interested
in both our physical and emotional health.
His goodness is available as a healing balm for
our sicknesses and emotional wounds. When
problems delay our hopes and plans, we can rest
assured God's goodness toward us will seem
even sweeter after a season of difficulties.

The Warmth of Hope

Hope deferred maketh the heart sick: but when
the desire cometh, it is a tree of life.

PROVERBS 13:12

Blooming in the Wilderness

Behold, I will do a new thing; now it shall spring forth;
shall ye not know it? I will even make a way in the
wilderness, and rivers in the desert.
ISAIAH 43:19

Cheryl bit off the thread. "Finished! Isn't it gorgeous?" She held up a quilted wall hanging for her husband to see.

"Ricky will love it." Ron looked at the meshing wheels appliquéd on the quilt. "This looks like interlocking gears, perfect for Ricky. Is there anything in this residence hall he hasn't taken apart since he's been a student here?"

Cheryl laughed. "Probably not. He won't have many graduation presents Saturday because he won't have family coming. I wanted him to have something to remember us by, as well as the Milton Hershey School. He has a promising future he never dreamed of before he came here."

"He'll make a good mark on society," Ron agreed.

"I'm glad we came here, too." Cheryl paused, and her eyes misted over. "After the baby died, the pain was so strong. I thought it was too much, like I'd never make it. But the hurt has eased since we took this job. Sometimes being houseparents has been a chore, but we've been able to contribute to the future of lots of kids." She smiled and slipped her hand into Ron's. "Now I feel like I'm stitching a little of my dreams for our own son into the life of another when I make these graduation quilts for our house boys."

Ron slid his arms around his wife. "I never imagined helping these boys and girls would heal our grief as well as it has. I love being part of an outreach to kids born into poor, hard situations. Our baby—" Ron stopped and cleared his throat. "He was such a fighter, despite the problems. I know he wanted to live. I feel now as if we've transferred that fight to these kids who will make a difference with their lives because they have learned how to study and squarely face life."

> **Scrap Basket**
> Renewed interest in quilting boomed because of the 1976 bicentennial. Public buildings around the nation displayed quilts because of their historical significance. The celebration drew attention to our American heritage and crafts, especially quilts.

God's Pattern

Out of the wildernesses of our lives, God will provide rivers of water. He will bring new vitality to the places in lives that are dry and barren. God heals every hurt when we stop replaying the loss over and over and, instead, ask Him to give us a new beginning.

The Warmth of Hope

Thou art my hiding place and my shield:
I hope in thy word.

PSALM 119:114

Rust Marks

*The lines are fallen unto me in pleasant places;
yea, I have a goodly heritage.*
PSALM 16:6

*L*ois wiped her eyes one last time, turned from her mother's fresh grave, and trudged to the waiting limousine. The sun peeked through the clouds, warming her back. To her surprise, the warmth spread to the chill in her heart.

"I believe I'll clean out Mother's cedar chest tomorrow. Want to help?" Lois asked her sister, Leslie, when they transferred from the funeral parlor's limousine to their own car.

Leslie raised her eyebrows. "Why on earth do you want to do that so soon?"

"Mother's sewing projects are in there. I want to look over her unfinished quilts. They bring good memories. We had some wonderful times together working on quilts."

Reluctantly Leslie agreed, and the next day, the sisters met at their mom's house. After a quick prayer, they went to the cedar chest and slowly opened the lid. The first thing they saw was a lovely Dresden

Plate quilt top, beautifully pieced with tiny hand stitching but only pinned to the batting and backing. "I think I'll finish this." Lois held it up for Leslie to see. "Mother wanted to finish it, but every time I offered to do it for her, she objected. She kept hoping she could finish it herself."

"But look, these pins have left rust marks." Leslie pulled out several pins, then paused. She sighed and pointed at tiny reddish brown dots on the backing wherever pins had held the layers together. "Rust. How sad. The marks spoil the whole quilt." Leslie put the comforter down. "No point in finishing a marred quilt."

> *Scrap Basket*
> **Storing quilts for a long time in contact with wood or acidic paper can cause brown stains.**

"I guess Mother pinned this together about the time the cancer first began, and she simply didn't have the energy to finish. The humid weather rusted the pins." Lois leaned over for a closer look at the rust marks that dotted the plain muslin. "I have an idea. Maybe I can embroider a little flower over each rust spot."

"Good idea," Leslie agreed.

"Pastel embroidery floss will blend with the floral fabric in the plates."

Lois packed the quilt carefully and took it home with her. A few weeks later, tiny flowers scattered over the plain muslin, and she went on to finish the quilting. She draped the unique Dresden Plate over her quilt stand, knowing she had fulfilled her mother's dream of finishing the quilt. "It's lovely in spite of the rust scars." Looking at it helped lift the heaviness Lois felt at the loss of her mother.

God's Pattern

God provided a way through His Son, Jesus, to take care of the blemishes sin leaves on our lives. When we repent and ask Jesus to become our Savior, God removes all trace of our sin. When we put God in charge of our hearts as our Lord, He embroiders beautiful designs on the fabric of our lives.

The Warmth of Hope

"You were wearied by all your ways, but you would not say, 'It is hopeless.' You found renewal of your strength, and so you did not faint."

ISAIAH 57:10 NIV

Brr!

Again, if two lie together, then they have heat:
but how can one be warm alone?
ECCLESIASTES 4:11

$\mathcal{A}$re you warm yet?" Hilda whispered to Ingrid, who huddled with her in the bed they shared in the drafty farmhouse.

"Not yet." Ingrid pulled several flannel quilts over her head.

"It's warmer when Winnie sleeps with us." Hilda tucked her feet up under her nightgown.

"Winnie went to sleep in Heidi and Gretchen's bed." Ingrid kept her voice low so the girls in bed on the other side of the room, divided by a hanging sheet, couldn't hear her. "She's mad at us because we ran away and hid when she asked us to help her card the wool for the new quilts."

"I don't like carding wool," Hilda said. "I'm always sticking my hands on those wire prongs more than I stick the wool I'm trying to separate and make fluffy. Besides, we don't have to do everything Winnie says just because she's the oldest." Hilda uncovered her eyes and glared her dissatisfaction with

Winnie. "Anyway, we did help cut out those big flannel squares, and we sewed them together."

"But if we had helped with the wool carding maybe we would have finished another quilt today for our bed, and we wouldn't be so cold." Ingrid scrunched closer to Hilda.

"Whoa, your feet are cold." Hilda moved away. "Put them under your nightgown like I do. We already have six quilts on our bed, but you're right. Another one would help on these cold nights."

"The Wagners have a stove that heats their house. I wish Papa thought it was safe to leave the fire roaring in the fireplace all night long," Ingrid said. "I'm going to help Winnie tomorrow. We can yarn tie a quilt in no time once the wool is ready for the middle."

> ### Scrap Basket
> Early settlers often needed quilts for warmth more than beauty. To speed up the completion of a blanket, large squares were cut from the fabrics available; then the three layers of the quilt were held together with yarn tied at each corner of the square.

"I guess I'll help, too." Hilda poked her head out from the covers and raised her voice. "Winnie, I'm sorry I didn't help with the wool carding. I will tomorrow. I know we need another quilt. It's awfully cold in here."

In a moment, a flannel-gowned figure slipped in beside Hilda. With the combined warmth, the three girls drifted off to sleep.

God's Pattern

The loneliness of broken relationships can be a
cold place. God designed our lives to strengthen
and sustain one another. Mending relationships
brings warmth and comfort back to our
lives, chasing the chill of loneliness away and
warming our hearts with companionship.

The Warmth of Hope

I wait for the LORD, my soul doth wait,
and in his word do I hope.

PSALM 130:5

Motorcycle Gloves

Confirming the souls of the disciples, and exhorting them to continue in the faith, and that we must through much tribulation enter into the kingdom of God.
ACTS 14:22

"What a stupid thing to do." Jenny stared at her right hand, freshly released from the cast. Surgery left angry red scars. "I *never* neglected wearing my gloves before when I rode my motorcycle," she told Sally, her therapist. Clenching her teeth, she tried to wiggle her fingers, alarm spreading over her face. "They won't move! It's like I put my hand in the freezer for a couple of months."

"The doctor did put your hand in a cast for a couple of months," Sally said. "Plus you've had skin grafts where you rubbed the skin off, skidding across the highway."

"The one time I'm careless would be the one time I had an accident."

"These things take time." Sally gently rubbed Jenny's palm. "I have an exercise for you."

Jenny winced as Sally began to tug at her fingers, and she drew back.

"This is a mental exercise," Sally reassured her. "I want you to set two goals you desire to accomplish as a result of your therapy. You need to establish in your mind why you're willing to endure the pain and push your limits to attain your goals."

"I want to be able to make a fist so I can grip a steering wheel and drive again."

"Good goal. Now give me another goal. You need two to keep you going."

"I want enough flexibility to sew again." Jenny loved to sew, and quilt almost as much as she loved that motorcycle. The thought of never being able to weave a shiny needle in and out again was almost too much. So she fought. And fought. Sometimes Jenny struggled so hard that sweat stood on her forehead. She shed many tears of frustration. She developed a rhythm to her therapy. Pray, move, and groan. Pray, move, and groan.

> **Scrap Basket**
> The early settlers worked hard to acquire the batting they used in their quilts. They sheared the sheep and then washed and carded the wool before it was ready to form the middle layer of a quilt.

Eventually, she brought the quilt she had begun before her accident to show Sally. When the months of struggle yielded a supple hand she could flex quickly in and out of a fist, she finished the quilt and gave it to Sally. "I never would have been able to sew again if you hadn't helped me."

God's Pattern

Often we participate in the miracles of our
lives. Instead of supernatural happenings, God
allows us to work hard to achieve our goals. The
fact we contribute doesn't mean our successes
are any less miraculous. He grants us the will
and ability to struggle and achieve. We also
need to set goals for our spiritual growth in
order to mature in our relationship with God.

The Warmth of Hope

Therefore did my heart rejoice,
and my tongue was glad; moreover
also my flesh shall rest in hope.

ACTS 2:26

Not for Wearing

*And whether one member suffer, all the members
suffer with it; or one member be honoured,
all the members rejoice with it.*

1 CORINTHIANS 12:26

"Would you look!" Where Emma had expected quilt hangings to be hung were rows upon rows of colorful bras.

Fern walked closer to the display at the quilt show. "What on earth?"

"Looks like fancy bras. Why are they hanging at a quilt show?" Emma wondered.

"Who would wear that?" Fern pointed to one bra with long, dangling strings of beads.

"Of all things, here's one with grapes on it."

"These can't be meant for wearing. Oh, my." Emma giggled. "Here's a stuffed old man and an old woman stitched onto a bra. You'd look lumpy if you wore this bulky thing under your clothes."

"Whimsy, but surely not to wear."

"Let's read the cards attached to them." Emma put on her glasses. "Now I get it. The purpose of this bra display is to honor women who died from breast cancer and those who beat the disease. The display is to remind us to have mammograms and raise research money."

Fern read a card. "This woman sewed the same number of pansies on her bra as the days she and her husband were married before he was shipped overseas to World War II. She put one little pansy in her husband's wallet to remind him of her during their separation."

> **Scrap Basket**
> Now most quilting is done by machine. New machines make it easier to quilt your own pieced quilt top.

"Sweet." The women made their way down the large display of numerous bras, all lavishly or outrageously decorated. They laughed, giggled, and sometimes made sympathetic noises when the card spoke of a woman's death from breast cancer.

"I suppose the fact large numbers of women attend quilt shows makes this an appropriate place to display the bra collection."

Fern grew pensive after reading another card. "I've never had a mammogram."

Emma looked at her friend in surprise. "Why not?"

"I've heard the machine hurts."

"What's a moment of pressure? The disease is much worse."

"But I'm afraid of the results. I don't want to deal with a bad report."

"Fern, think about it. Breast cancer is often cured if it's caught in time. A mammogram can catch it early. Goodness, girl, you are my best friend. Go have the exam for me if you won't do it for yourself. I want to keep you around for a long time."

God's Pattern

Encourage your friends to get mammograms
and other preventative medical procedures.
Remind them of their value to God and to you.

The Warmth of Hope

And our hope for you is firm, because we know
that just as you share in our sufferings, so also
you share in our comfort.

2 CORINTHIANS 1:7 NIV

Underground Railroad

*These things speak, and exhort, and rebuke
with all authority. Let no man despise thee.*
TITUS 2:15

*G*ood job." Miss Karen admired Keith's artwork.
He was copying onto paper one fabric square from
Miss Karen's Underground Railroad quilt. The quilt
hung on the back wall of her special-needs classroom.
Keith finished with a summary of the information
the square offered to the slave who wanted freedom.

"Which way do the quilt triangles point?" Miss
Karen asked.

"Straight up," Keith answered.

"What did that tell a slave who wanted to connect with the Underground Railroad?"

"To walk north." Keith held up his paper. "See,
three triangles, then brown material that looks like a
house tells slaves to walk three miles north to a safe
house."

"Tell us about your square, Tracy," Miss Karen
requested.

"My square shows dogs with teeth on the right
side of the quilt." Tracy pointed. "That means a slave

shouldn't go to the east where dogs might chase and corner him."

Miss Karen smiled. Tim scanned the pictures into the computer as the children finished them. Tim's stuttering didn't affect his preparation of the computer presentation. The entire school watched the computer program about the Underground Railroad unit.

The special-needs class, dressed in their best, sat on the platform for the computerized slide show. As a computer square appeared, Tim pointed to the corresponding one in the real quilt.

The pictures and captions told stories of families facing dangers to escape slavery. Miss Karen's students chose music to reflect the tension of the

> ### Scrap Basket
> Although experts disagree about whether quilts were used as signals to convey information to escaping slaves, we do know sympathetic people helped slaves travel to freedom.

stories. A brass band played music for the last scene of a man welcomed to a safe city. The auditorium erupted in applause when the program ended. The class beamed from the rare public praise. More accustomed to jokes and teasing, the kids gained confidence from the success of the program.

"Good job," the principal said, then asked the class to stand. Miss Karen's smile was the broadest one of all.

God's Pattern

When others scorn us, we can draw comfort
from knowing that if we follow God's plan, our
sense of worth will follow. Hard work brings
the reward of confidence more than empty
words of praise where no effort was required.
Persistent work enlarges our capacity for more
effort and leads to attaining goals. Rather than
stew about how others view us and worry about
our perceived handicaps, realize it is God's
opinion of us that counts. Then work
hard as He directs.

The Warmth of Hope

For evil men will be cut off, but those who
hope in the LORD will inherit the land.

PSALM 37:9 NIV

Teddy Bear Ball

*To every thing there is. . .a time to weep, and a time
to laugh; a time to mourn, and a time to dance.*
ECCLESIASTES 3:4

I want to bid on the quilt." Melita spoke near her
husband's ear, and her silver-slippered feet followed
his lead, swooping and whirling through a perfect
waltz.

Ian smiled at his wife, elegant in her emerald
satin gown. Her diamond earrings flashed in the
lights of the ballroom. "Of course. That's the purpose of the Teddy Bear Ball. Raise money for the
children's clinic."

"Yes, but I really want to win it. I want to take
one of those three separate sections home and hang
it over the fireplace."

"And?" Ian tucked his wife's head closer to his
shoulder. "What do you propose to do with the other
two sections of the quilt?"

"Why, donate them to the clinic, of course. We'll
frame them and hang them across from the elevators
where they will welcome everyone who comes."

"How much do you think we need to bid to

win the quilt, since it's in three parts this year?" Ian twirled Melita under his arm.

"That's your area of expertise. You know what it takes to win."

Ian planted a kiss on Melita's forehead. "Are you sure you want to put our money into a quilt raffle rather than a trip to the jeweler for, say, a diamond necklace to match your earrings?"

"I see those brave children who come week after week to the clinic, hoping some medical miracle will ease their suffering or lengthen their lives. Helping those families is the kind of necklace I want, the decorating ornament I desire for my life. Tonight is our time to dance and laugh—and to help those who are troubled."

God's Pattern
To those to whom much is given, much is required. To decorate our lives with service to others pleases God and brings us gladness.

The Warmth of Hope
The hope of the righteous shall be gladness.
PROVERBS 10:28

Bells of Grace

To the praise of the glory of his grace, wherein
he hath made us accepted in the beloved.
EPHESIANS 1:6

*A*nswer the door, child," Grandma requested.

Cora dropped the green beans she and Grandma were snapping into the basin of water on the table. She loved answering the door at Grandma's house. Silver bells tinkled whenever the door moved. Their merry sound sent cheer throughout the house.

She opened the door but did not invite their guest in. "It's Mrs. Winter!" Cora called over her shoulder. Then she grinned as she swung the door back and forth.

"I'm coming." Wiping her hands, Grandma hurried to usher her guest into the living room.

"This child needs manners," Mrs. Winter told Grandma. "The idea—keeping me standing at the door."

Cora continued to fan the door. A concert of jingling bells delighted her ears.

Mrs. Winter glared. "Stop that racket."

Grandma's voice was more gentle. "Close the

door, Cora, and come meet Mrs. Winter."

Cora sat, bored, while the women talked about making quilts for wounded war veterans who were coming home from France. Cora wished Mrs. Winter would leave. She wanted to snap beans and listen to Grandma talk about her childhood, and she kept thinking about Mrs. Winter's glare. Maybe she *had* been rude. Cora sat up straighter. Maybe Mrs. Winter would like her better if she saw her helping. Cora ran to the kitchen and returned with the basin of soaking beans. She sat at the other end of the sofa from Mrs. Winter and began to snap the beans.

> **Scrap Basket**
> Elaborate quilts
> like Baltimore
> Album quilts were
> often used only for
> guest beds.

"Stop that! Your snap, snap, snap is distracting," Mrs. Winter complained.

Disappointed, Cora leaped up to go back to the kitchen, but she moved too fast, dumping the entire pan, water and all, over the sofa and a good portion on Mrs. Winter. The woman jumped to her feet. "Well, I'll be—" she sputtered.

"I'll make three quilts for our soldiers." Grandma snatched her own quilt off a chair to soak up the water.

"I should hope. Keep a firm hand on that one. She's a pistol." Mrs. Winter pointed to Cora and left.

At bedtime, an electric fan dried the sofa cushions. Keyed up from her encounter with Mrs. Winter,

Cora couldn't sleep. To relax her, Grandma wrapped her in another quilt and brushed her hair.

"Did the quilt get ruined?"

"No," Grandma answered. "Don't you worry. Things are for using. Don't be one of those people who save things for special occasions only. Most of the time, those occasions never occur, and the item, too lovely to use, is never enjoyed. Use the quilt I made you."

Cora curled her arms around Grandma. "I'm sorry about Mrs. Winter. Do you still love me?"

"Of course I love you. You are my beloved grand-child. Things are to use. People are to love."

It was a lesson Cora never forgot. Today Cora keeps Grandma's bells on her own door to remind her of God's grace—and her grandmother's love.

God's Pattern

God's grace makes us accepted in the family of God because we believe in Jesus, not because of our own merits or others' opinions of us.

The Warmth of Hope

Through whom also we have obtained our introduction by faith into this grace in which we stand; and we exult in hope of the glory of God.

ROMANS 5:2 NASB

Fair Days

And the King shall answer and say unto them, Verily I say unto you, Inasmuch as ye have done it unto one of the least of these my brethren, ye have done it unto me.
MATTHEW 25:40

W ow! It's hot." Michelle wiped her forehead.

"You can say that again," Lena agreed. "My sweaty fingers keep sticking to the yarn." Lena pulled red yarn through the quilt and tied a knot.

A small crowd gathered around the girls to see what they were doing. The large quilt frame made an effective eye-catcher at the county fair. "Wanna buy a raffle ticket for the big quilt?" Lena asked, pointing to a king-sized Log Cabin quilt hanging behind the girls.

She collected several dollars in exchange for raffle tickets.

"Are you raffling off this one, too?" Mr. Jeffreys fingered the quilt the girls were tying.

"No," answered Lena. "We're donating this quilt to the shelter for abused women. Quilts comfort the little children living there."

"Yeah," Michelle chimed in. "They can't understand why Mommy is afraid of Daddy and why, all of a sudden, they are living somewhere else. We make them quilts to cuddle. The raffle is for our 4-H Club expenses."

Ria arrived. "I saw a little boy at the shelter rubbing a quilt against his chin and sucking his thumb. He looked like he was about to cry." She sat down at the quilt frame. "I'm ready to help. How are we doing so far?"

"We've tied six quilts." Michelle pointed to the pile on a table. "We have seven more to go."

Scrap Basket
In the early 1800s, dame schools required girls to bring their patchwork to school.

"What industrious girls!" exclaimed Mr. Jeffreys. "Do you have a set time you must work in your booth?"

"We drop by whenever we can and tie the layers together as fast as possible."

"We sewed the squares together at our 4-H Club meetings before the fair began."

"You girls are amazing," Mr. Jeffreys said. "I'll buy twenty tickets for the raffle."

While Michelle counted out the tickets, Ria began working. "With three of us, we should get one more quilt tied together before suppertime."

Michelle's mother, Mrs. Thomas, came by. "You girls have spent a lot of hours out here today. I brought some cold drinks."

"Thanks," Lena said. "It's worth it, hot and sticky and all. I saw firsthand how those little kids at the abused women's shelter cuddle quilts. I'm glad you showed us how to make quilts, Mrs. Thomas."

"Feels good to help someone, doesn't it?" Mrs. Thomas replied.

God's Pattern
When we help others, we are helping someone God loves, which pleases God and brings us satisfaction. He created each person with great care.

The Warmth of Hope
Now the God of hope fill you with all joy and peace in believing, that ye may abound in hope, through the power of the Holy Ghost.

ROMANS 15:13

Quilt Drama

Be thou exalted, LORD, in thine own strength:
so will we sing and praise thy power.
PSALM 21:13

Silence blanketed the old barn when the final song faded into the rafters. Then thunderous applause punctuated with shouts of "Bravo! Bravo!" filled the theater. Ava wiped her eyes. A sniffle to her right and left confirmed that Lori and Tara felt the same emotional tug as she. The entire audience seemed reluctant to leave the production's stirring portrayal of pioneer quilters for the reality of the present day. The quilt from the play's finale still hung on the stage.

Tara took a deep breath. "I wonder what drives us to fill our lives with such color and song."

"That's easy," Ava answered. "God did. God gives us a love for beauty, our desire to create loveliness. He gave us that drive to help us throw ourselves into extravagant worship of Him. We can dance around our house and fill it with our songs of praise. Our love of beauty gives us varied ways to worship Him. Unfortunately, our society has switched the purpose to striving for fun and games." She grinned. "Let's get a closer look at that spectacular quilt."

"I love the bold colors," Tara said. "Using the origins of quilt patterns was a clever way to tie together scenes about pioneer life. Makes me appreciate pioneer women. Settling the West was dangerous and arduous."

"Not to mention lonely," Lori added. "We don't appreciate today's blessings enough. Craving beauty is universal, regardless of time and place."

"I didn't realize how much pioneer women longed to put a splash of color in their lives," Ava agreed.

> *Scrap Basket*
> The beauty and color of quilts helped the isolated pioneer woman maintain mental health. The renaissance of quilting today is driven by the desire to create beauty.

"I think quilting still satisfies the same needs today: warmth, color, and a connection to the past." Ava blew her nose. "A longing to be remembered, to make our life count. Quilts are still a way to express yourself."

"The patterns in the play's quilt represented heartaches and victories," Tara said. "It's not much different for us. Both our heartaches and our triumphs influence our quilt designs."

"Makes me want to learn to quilt," Lori said.

Tara brightened, offering up the invitation. "Come with us to our quilt guild. We can make some of our own beauty."

God's Pattern

Our creative urges are given to us by God to
draw us to Him and help us worship Him in
many ways and learn about His many facets.
The ultimate goal of this life is to grow more
like Jesus and more adept at praising Him.

The Warmth of Hope

But I will hope continually, and will
yet praise thee more and more.

PSALM 71:14

Rescued

Fear ye not therefore, ye are of more
value than many sparrows.
MATTHEW 10:31

"Here, Goldie! Come on!" Janey tried out another common name for golden retrievers. The dog ignored her. "She must have a name," Janey told her husband. "She's obviously been well cared for, and she's affectionate with people."

"She also shows definite signs of post-traumatic stress. Look how she sticks next to you like she's glued there." Mike looked at their foster dog. "Poor animal. No telling what she went through before she was rescued from the floods in New Orleans. No wonder she's afraid of separation and confining places."

Suddenly the dog perked up and took off after a bird. "No! Lady!" Janey called. The dog stopped in her tracks, snapped her head around, and trotted back to Janey. "Look at that. I'll bet her family named her Lady." Janey rubbed the dog, whose fur had been shaved from the bottom half of her body. Lady had arrived at the local shelter, coated with black goo from the hurricane floodwaters.

Janey sighed as the dog took her place once more at Janey's side. "I hope the Web search finds her owners. She's been a beloved pet. Even the way she took to our fancy quilted dog bed makes me think she was used to a comfortable quilt in her New Orleans home before the hurricane."

Mike scratched the golden retriever's ears. "Either she's accustomed to the comfort of quilts or she's determined not to let us out of her sight, and the quilted dog bed is beside our bed."

> **Scrap Basket**
> Quilts rescue fabric scraps that would otherwise be discarded. Quilts offer comfort to the traumatized, the fearful, the lost.

"I hope we can find her owners, but I'm glad we're foster caretakers for her while the search goes on. I like helping poor, traumatized animals."

"I'd never have guessed!" Mike grinned as three other rescued dogs bounded up to lick their hands. "Even the potbellied pig is oinking his agreement."

God's Pattern

The God who sees the fall of every
sparrow is the God who plants His love
in human hearts to treat animals with
tenderness and compassion. God desires we
show even more tender compassion for his
treasured creation—humans. If His tenderness
includes our animals, how much more does
it apply to us! He comforts the lost and brings
the fearful into the family of God. The
security and love found in church allows
people to heal from traumatic experiences.

The Warmth of Hope

"So there is hope for your future,"
declares the LORD. "Your children
will return to their own land."

JEREMIAH 31:17 NIV

Kid Comfort

*Be strong and of a good courage, fear not, nor be afraid
of them: for the LORD thy God, he it is that doth go with
thee; he will not fail thee, nor forsake thee.*
DEUTERONOMY 31:6

*L*ook at these pictures." Jackie held up fabric pictures made from snapshots. The pictures showed a
family playing at the beach, riding bumper cars, and
posing for the camera.

"Touches your heart, doesn't it?" Bev stitched
around similar pictures on another quilt.

"While I sew, I pray this dad comes safely back
to his family." Jackie fingered one of the pictures.
"Doesn't he look strong in his army fatigues?"

"Operation Kid Comfort is great. But quilts for
kids with parents deployed far away is a poor substi-
tute for a real hug" Alyssa said.

Bev took a deep breath, saying a quick prayer for
her husband, who was safe at work. "Makes you stop
and think about the time we fuss and fume with our
families at home."

Alyssa made a wry face. "Like sending Tom off
to work this morning with a lecture about carrying

his fair share of the responsibilities."

Jackie offered understanding. "It's reasonable to be upset because he isn't trying to get a better job."

"But he comes home every night. He cares about what happens to me and the kids. He holds me when I'm afraid, like the night Freddy broke his arm. I was so upset I was shaking." She sighed. "And this little boy has to settle for hugging a quilt. My Freddy had his daddy hugging him. What does it matter, anyhow, how much money he makes? God hasn't failed us. We have everything we need, not all our wants, but our needs. I need to trust God and His promises."

Carla came in, carrying bundles of batting. "I'm glad you ladies are making quilts for Operation Kid Comfort. I can't sew on a button without tangling the thread, but my company likes donating the materials you need."

God's Pattern

Even small acts of kindness can
encourage faith in difficult situations.
When we show we care about people's troubles,
we help them keep a grip on their trust in God.
We help their courage while they wait to see
how God will help them in their battle. God
does not fail us even in difficult times.
He brings us through trials, wrapped in His
love as a quilt wraps us in warmth.

The Warmth of Hope

But Christ is faithful as a son over God's house.
And we are his house, if we hold on to our
courage and the hope of which we boast.

HEBREWS 3:6 NIV

Sacks and Bullets

For the weapons of our warfare are not carnal,
but mighty through God to the pulling
down of strong holds.
2 Corinthians 10:4

Mildred jumped when the clanging bell signaled quitting time to dozens of women stitching heavy canvas sacks. Planting a hand on top of her black sewing machine, she pulled herself up.

From the next machine, Ruby reached a hand out. "Mildred, give me a tug."

Mildred helped her friend stand, and Ruby kneaded the small of her back with her hands. "Why do I drag myself in here every day to sit, sewing hundreds of boring sacks 'til I'm so stiff I can't even stand up?"

"Same reason I do." Mildred stretched, easing the kinks out of her legs. "For the soldiers. These sacks hold munitions to help them stay alive."

"I know. Our troops are keeping the war away from our land, but when I go home, I think that World War II has crossed the ocean and invaded my living room," Ruby grumbled. She took her place in line behind Mildred to punch their time cards. "Sometimes I think Gene argues just for the sake of arguing. It's one disagreement after another. Last night, he got mad because I worked on my quilt."

"Tell you what," Mildred said. "Let's have dinner together this weekend. We can pool our meat ration coupons and make a nice meat loaf. Tell Gene that Ken and I'll come over early and help weed. Pull-

> **Scrap Basket**
> During World War II, more women began to work outside the home to help with the war effort. These jobs, as well as knitting and making bandages for the Red Cross, competed with time to quilt.

ing trash out of your victory garden should work out some ornery attitudes. I'll bring my quilt, and while the men talk after dinner, you and I can go to your sewing room. We'll stitch and pray. Maybe that will help the atmosphere in your house."

"I'm just as bad as Gene. I can't stop complaining."

"Don't give up." Mildred gave Ruby an encouraging hug. "You have a greater weapon than the munitions these sacks hold. Your weapon is the power of God to overcome regrettable attitudes and habits. Together, we'll pray and tear down those strongholds in our lives."

God's Pattern

Instead of feeling discouraged with our weaknesses and those of others, remember that the war is not a battle of the flesh but a battle of the spirit. We don't need to fight our battles alone. When we realize certain reactions or attitudes are destructive, God will help us overcome our weaknesses and change to new ways. God overcomes our enemies.

The Warmth of Hope

For the hope which is laid up for you in heaven, whereof ye heard before in the word of the truth of the gospel.

COLOSSIANS 1:5

Toad

*To appoint unto them that mourn in Zion, to give
unto them beauty for ashes, the oil of joy for mourning,
the garment of praise for the spirit of heaviness; that
they might be called trees of righteousness, the planting
of the LORD, that he might be glorified.*
ISAIAH 61:3

Delores ran to embrace her sister and niece, Patricia and Hillary, when she disembarked from the airplane in Copenhagen, Denmark. She hugged them both tightly, and Patricia's tears flowed as they walked to the parking garage. "I can't think straight since Jeff drowned." Patricia's hands shook as they wandered around trying to locate her car, and she almost dropped the keys trying to open it. "At least we think he drowned," Patricia continued, as she drove to her home in the suburbs. "It's awful not knowing how he died."

Listening to the depth of her sister's grief for her son, Delores was glad she made the long trip from North Carolina to spend time with her devastated family. She sat quietly, letting her sister vent her frustration and pain.

"I just don't understand. He made other sailing

trips to Mexico. Jeff always obeyed his dad's instructions to not venture out of sight of land when he sailed. Maybe he happened upon some smuggling drug lord who murdered him." Patricia shuddered.

At the house, Delores unpacked, then presented Patricia and Hillary with the quilt she had made in response to the family tragedy.

"I can't believe it!" Hillary clapped a hand over her mouth at the sight of green frogs cavorting over a turquoise background. "Auntie, I'll bet you didn't know Jeffie's nickname for me was Toad. This is the perfect memory quilt. I'll think of his teasing whenever I see it." She sighed and held the quilt to her face. "He was a neat brother."

> **Scrap Basket**
> Although space was limited when pioneers moved west, they included quilts in their packing as objects of comfort when separated from family back east.

A few days later, a letter from Mexico began the road to discovery and healing. Jeff had stopped at the coastal property of a couple who befriended him, fed him, and took his picture, which they enclosed. The letter extolled him as a fine young man and expressed hope he had arrived home safely. Patricia called the people. Now they had a date to help the authorities know the last time Jeff was seen. The couple circulated flyers, which resulted in someone contacting them. Finally, the Mexican police found Jeff's body.

Patricia and her husband made a trip to Mexico

and visited the family who had last seen Jeff. They returned comforted by the knowledge that his death was an accident, not foul play.

Hillary hung the frog quilt as a constant reminder of the love she had shared with her brother. Slowly their pain began to heal.

God's Pattern
People experience unbelievable grief in
this fallen world; yet, as impossible as
it seems, God brings comfort and peace.
Our responsibility is to recognize His care
for us and allow our souls to receive His
comfort in whatever form it comes.

The Warmth of Hope
The wicked is driven away in his wickedness:
but the righteous hath hope in his death.
PROVERBS 14:32

Licks

Then washed I thee with water; yea,
I thoroughly washed away thy blood from thee,
and I anointed thee with oil.
EZEKIEL 16:9

"Tonight, I'm going to start quilting. That's my new hobby. I'll watch TV and quilt," Linda told her sister on the phone. "I love the bold colors of the flannels I'm using." She braced the phone against her shoulder and set her basket on her lap, admiring the fabric colors. "I've already sewn the pieces together. Yesterday, I drew the pattern for my quilting stitches over the whole quilt with an erasable marker."

When Linda hung up, she settled back on the sofa, turned on the TV, and invited Rusty, her cocker spaniel, onto her lap. Rusty settled onto the soft quilt fabric, resting his head on her leg with a sigh. The forensic drama grabbed her attention, and she stitched away, alternating her glances between the screen and the quilt.

"Phew, Rusty, too much tension for me." Linda turned off the TV when the program ended. "Bedtime." She stood, dumping Rusty off her lap and onto the floor. When she began to fold her quilt, she gave it a closer look. "Rusty, you little rascal, you. You've licked off all the marks for my quilting. Here I thought you were giving yourself an especially long bath." Linda didn't know whether to laugh or cry.

"Instead, you were licking my quilt." She felt the quilt. "Damp. Incriminating evidence, you little scoundrel."

Rusty looked at her and wagged his tail. "Serves me right, marking the whole thing at once. I've learned my lesson. With you around, my little friend, I'll mark only one section at a time." Linda spread the quilt over the end of the couch so it could dry, then scooped Rusty up and carried him toward the bedroom as the happy pooch squirmed and licked her face.

> **Scrap Basket**
> Quilt-show judges don't want to see animal hair on a quilt.

God's Pattern

Erasable markers help quilters draw complicated patterns to guide their stitches. The marks remove easily with cold water. When Christians choose destructive patterns of living, it's as if they mar their lives with marks that need erasing. God will forgive us when we ask and will help us stitch better patterns into our lives. He will erase the guilt when we repent. The Ezekiel scripture above foreshadows God's

cleansing of those who believe Jesus is the Son
of God who died for our sins.

The Warmth of Hope

For to him that is joined to all the living there is
hope: for a living dog is better than a dead lion.

ECCLESIASTES 9:4

Restored

*And Jesus answered and said unto them, Elias truly
shall first come, and restore all things.*
MATTHEW 17:11

Maria burst into the house, sobbing. "Mom,
Dustin is dying!"

"What happened?" Iris folded her daughter
within her arms. Thoughts of Maria's days of dating Dustin swirled while she tried to sort the facts
from Maria's hysterical account. A car accident that
morning had put Dustin in intensive care, fighting
for his life.

"Are you sorry you broke up with him?" Iris asked
when Maria's sobs subsided to hiccups.

"No, his parents hate me. They didn't want us
dating. But I didn't want him to die!" she finished
with a wail.

"Hate is a strong word. It wasn't you. They weren't
ready for their son to start dating anyone." Iris tried
to comfort her child. *But they have been cool to her.*

When a phone call confirmed Dustin was in
danger, Iris went to her fabric stash. "Maria, I'm going to make a small flannel quilt and take it to the

hospital tomorrow. Do you want to come?"

"Yes. He's still my friend, and I want to see him. I'd feel less awkward having you with me."

Iris stayed up late and sewed flannel squares together. She sewed the raw edges to the front side to make a fringelike decoration. With some trepidation, she and Maria took the quilt to the ICU the next day. The pair entered the hospital and asked permission to visit Dustin. When Dustin's parents came out immediately, Iris held out the quilt.

"You can come back and give it to him yourself." Mrs. Brown hugged Iris, then Maria, and led the way. She laid the flannel quilt over Dustin's feet. "Doesn't it look like he relaxed a bit at the warmth?" she asked Maria hopefully.

> **Scrap Basket**
> Today's women often buy fabric because it's beautiful and to keep on hand to use for the unanticipated project.

Iris returned the next day with sandwiches so Dustin's parents could eat without leaving their son. She and Maria visited frequently, hugging the Browns and praying with them, admiring how their hope remained strong. But Dustin's condition continued to deteriorate.

In the days before Dustin's death, Iris found little things to do for the Browns while they grieved together about his condition. Mrs. Brown told her more than once how much it meant to them, how much the quilt meant to the aching parents.

Iris finally realized how much when Maria came back from visiting them, just after Dustin died. "Mom," she said, holding her mother, "the Browns want to put your quilt over the foot of the casket."

God's Pattern

People's emotions are closer to the surface when experiencing trauma and dealing with death. Acts of kindness make a greater impact during such times. God uses these difficult circumstances, those times when we are most vulnerable, to draw us closer to Himself.

The Warmth of Hope

I eagerly expect and hope that I will in no way be ashamed, but will have sufficient courage so that now as always Christ will be exalted in my body, whether by life or by death.

PHILIPPIANS 1:20 NIV

Life's Translation

And how shall they preach, except they be sent?
as it is written, How beautiful are the feet of them
that preach the gospel of peace, and bring
glad tidings of good things!
ROMANS 10:15

*A*h." Howtung acknowledged the request from Rosalind, the president of the quilt guild. He spoke quickly to his wife, Paling. Although the women close by didn't understand a word he said, they smiled, enjoying the musical lilt of his Chinese.

Paling stood and carried her quilt forward for her turn to show and tell about her completed quilt. Paling held one corner as her husband held the other, his face alight with his proud smile. "See." He pointed. "Wife put ten panda bears on quilt. Panda bears from our country. She, what you say. . . ? She sewed around edges with her hand. Ah, she. . . ," Howtung faltered, trying to find the right words. In response to the chorus of voices supplying him with the unfamiliar word, he said, "Appliqué!" He took another deep breath. "She makes tiny, little stitches when she quilts. Very good, okay?"

The women applauded. "Tell Paling her choices of color and fabric combinations are beautiful," Rosalind instructed. Paling flushed after her husband relayed the message in Chinese, and the couple returned to their seats at a nearby table.

One of the guild members stood to give instructions on how to use a special ruler. Howtung quietly translated the directions for his wife. Although Paling didn't speak any English, she had been coming to the guild for a year. Brought to the United States by a technology firm, Howtung faithfully accompanied her and translated.

Delighted by Paling and her husband's faithful attendance, Rosalind yearned to tell them the story of Jesus. She decided that night to make a quilt, with each square representing an aspect of Jesus' ministry on earth. She hoped her own show-and-tell would be an opportunity to expose the couple to Jesus and His redemption for eternity. Rosalind knew that the enthusiastic love each guild member showed the couple translated the gospel to the quiet people even better than her quilt would when she explained it. She hoped the quilt would plant pictures of Christ's love.

> **Scrap Basket**
> The love of quilts and the process of quilting transcend international boundaries. Every year, people from many countries around the world attend the Houston International Quilt Festival.

God's Pattern

When people show love to others in concrete
ways, they are a living translation of the Bible
story. Sometimes people comprehend the
meaning of the gospel better through loving
actions than through preaching. However, God
wants us to be prepared to explain the gospel
as well as demonstrate it. God directs us to be
ready to explain the reason we have hope in this
world.

The Warmth of Hope

But sanctify the Lord God in your hearts: and
be ready always to give an answer to every man
that asketh you a reason of the hope that is in
you with meekness and fear.

1 PETER 3:15

Generations

Know therefore that the LORD thy God, he is God,
the faithful God, which keepeth covenant and
mercy with them that love him and keep his
commandments to a thousand generations.
DEUTERONOMY 7:9

*J*asmine bit her lip as she stitched two three-inch squares together.

"Good job." Grandma examined her seam. "After you sew the third square across, we'll stitch three more below, making sure you alternate the pink floral squares with the blue ones. With a third row below the second, you'll have finished a nine patch, and you are on your way to being a quilter."

Jasmine beamed and lowered the presser foot to sew a pink-striped square next to the blue one.

"Looks like a productive morning," Paula, Jasmine's mother, said later when she returned from her dental appointment.

"I'm a quilter. Grandma says so." Jasmine held up her nine-patch square.

"You did a better job than I did when I was

your age." Paula looked at the completed square and hugged her daughter. "Mother, do you remember the first couple of nine-patch squares you had me make to get used to using the sewing machine?"

"Indeed I do. I have them right here packed away in this box with the ones my mother instructed me to make when I was Jasmine's age." She opened the box and laid out Paula's squares on the table. Next to them, she spread out the ones she made herself when she was a girl.

"What else is in the box?" Paula asked.

"These are the nine-patch squares my mother made when she was a girl, learning to sew."

> ### Scrap Basket
> For female companionship, today's quilt classes and quilt guilds replace the quilting bees of long ago.

"Do you realize what a treasure we have?" Paula lined the squares up next to one another. "When Jasmine makes two more squares, we'll have enough to make a quilt."

"A four-generation quilt. How special!"

Paula took the squares with her, and as Jasmine watched, she sewed a strip of coordinating material between each nine-patch square. She then showed her daughter how to make the tiny stitches to bond the three layers of the quilt. Together they quilted the generation project. A sense of family security and continuity now blankets Jasmine when she sleeps under the quilt spread on her antique bed.

God's Pattern

God desires to bless each generation in a family.
The most important heritage we can leave
our family is the love of God and a desire
to serve Him. His blessing rests on generation
after generation where the name of Jesus
is revered and worshiped.

The Warmth of Hope

For there is hope of a tree, if it be cut down,
that it will sprout again, and that the tender
branch thereof will not cease.

JOB 14:7

The Price

You see that his faith and his actions were working together, and his faith was made complete by what he did.
JAMES 2:22 NIV

"Would you like to put your signature and thumbprint on this quilt?" Miriam asked each approaching guest. The women were there to attend the church's annual ladies' luncheon. Miriam, stunning in her black suit highlighted by the clean lines of gold jewelry, stood by an equally stunning quilt in shades of pink and rose and dotted with small, plain muslin squares appropriate for signatures.

"There is a fee to sign my quilt," she explained to them. "The price is a mammogram. The quilt will be here for several weeks. Come back with an appointment card for a mammogram, and you can sign and put your thumbprint on this important quilt. It will hang here in the fellowship hall to remind women to get a mammogram. A mammogram can save your life."

"It saved mine," one lady piped up to the guests who had clustered around the lovely quilt. "There's my signature right there." She pointed to the upper left-hand corner. "My mammogram showed a suspicious spot. I didn't have a clue anything was wrong and would not have remembered to make an appointment if it had not been required to sign this quilt. A lumpectomy, some radiation, and I'm good as new, ready for many more years."

Miriam beamed. "Valuable years, if they are anything like the love you've offered thus far." This wasn't the first testimony from someone who had conquered breast cancer before it got out of control. For years, Miriam's passion to prevent death from breast cancer led her to make quilts and ask women to pay for the privilege to sign them by having a mammogram. Her quilts, ranging in size from wall hangings to king-size bed quilts, hung in many buildings around her area, reminding women to take control of their health and have regular checkups, including mammograms.

> ### Scrap Basket
> The early feminist movement looked down on homemaking chores, which made quilting unfashionable for a time.

God's Pattern
God inspires all the medical advances of our society, whether the scientists recognize God's influence or not. We are using God-inspired techniques when we combine a trust in God's protection with preventative and early diagnostic medical measures.

The Warmth of Hope

Therefore, prepare your minds for action; be
self-controlled; set your hope fully on the grace
to be given you when Jesus Christ is revealed.

1 PETER 1:13 NIV

Bandannas of Love

*And above all things have fervent charity among
yourselves: for charity shall cover the multitude of sins.*
1 PETER 4:8

Wigs are hot, and hats are prickly on my bald
head. They feel weird in a lot of places where I go."
Sue unleashed her frustrations with her cancer and
her baldness to her friend over the phone. Heather
was the kind of friend she could be honest with
about everything. "I bought a bandanna. It feels good
and covers my shining bald head well, but it's so un-
feminine. I don't want to wear jeans every time I go
to church just so I can match the style and mood of
a cowboy bandanna."

When Heather hung up from talking on the
phone to her friend, who lived several states away,
she went straight to her fabric store and bought an
assortment of soft fabrics in varied colors, including
some feminine prints. At home, she cut out triangles
and sewed bandannas. She edged the one cut from
white damask with lace and embroidered another
with birds. Every week she mailed her friend another
bandanna to cover her head. She supplied the gifts,

ranging from casual to dressy, until Sue finished her chemotherapy.

"My favorite, so far, is the one with three colors of silk braided and tacked to the long side of the triangle," Sue told her later. "I wear that whenever I wear my silk dress."

Inspired by so much leftover material in triangular shapes, Heather pieced together a quilt top from the fabrics. About the time she was ready to quilt the top, her own mammogram came back showing a suspicious area. She quilted furiously during the days of testing and waiting. She prayed just as feverishly, inspired by Sue's courage and determination.

> *Scrap Basket*
> Triangles are the foundation shape for many varied and interesting quilt designs.

Heather told her so in a note she sent to accompany the finished quilt she mailed to Sue. "Making this quilt has been good therapy while the doctors examine my condition. I'm confident I can handle whatever happens because I've been a part of your fight against breast cancer."

Both women rejoiced when Heather's tests turned out negative. Sue fully recovered, and the women continue to enjoy their friendship.

God's Pattern

In modern translations of the Bible, *charity* is translated *love*. When we love someone, we will not expose a person's failings to others. Instead, we cover for them by not thinking— or talking—negatively about them. Heather literally covered the temporary physical awkwardness of Sue's baldness from chemotherapy by making head coverings for her friend. Likewise, we cover for our friends when we choose to believe the kindest interpretation of their actions and words. In our love, we can give our friends the benefit of believing in them and praying for them.

The Warmth of Hope

It is good that a man should both hope and quietly wait for the salvation of the LORD.

LAMENTATIONS 3:26

The Bird Lady

But now thus saith the LORD that created thee,
O Jacob, and he that formed thee, O Israel, Fear not:
for I have redeemed thee, I have called thee by
thy name; thou art mine.
ISAIAH 43:1

I love it." Joanne examined a particularly lovely top on sale at Mia's quilt-show booth. "I can't resist buying this." Joanne opened her purse. "I love the beautiful bird on the corner."

"Birds are this woman's trademark. She puts a large bird somewhere on every quilt top she makes. We call her The Bird Lady of Paducah. I sell lots of her quilt tops."

"I can see why. She's a master of primitive art."

"Come back next year. I hope to have more of The Bird Lady's quilts," Mia said.

The next year, Joanne couldn't wait for the show to open, and on the first day, she made a beeline for Mia's booth. "I'm ready to buy another of The Bird Lady of Paducah's quilt tops."

Mia sighed. "I don't have any."

"How can that be? I came straight here when the

festival opened."

"It's a mystery. She's disappeared."

Joanne gasped. "Nothing happened to her, did it?"

"No one has seen her. Since not one of the vendors had heard from her, some of us went to her house where we've picked up quilts before. Imagine our surprise to see the house isn't there anymore. It's torn down, and the lot is empty."

"Did she leave a forwarding address at the post office?"

"We tried to find out, but I'm embarrassed to say no one

> ### Scrap Basket
> Quilt labels tell the name of the quilter and the date the quilt was made, adding to a quilt's historical significance.

knows her name. She was simply The Bird Lady of Paducah. We can't trace her. That's the strangest part. We're all wondering what happened to her."

Joanne couldn't hide her disappointment. "I wanted to buy another piece of her work."

"And I wanted to sell more of her quilt tops. At least you have the satisfaction of owning the last piece she made for us."

"Maybe she went to live with a grown child. If so, her quilts might show up again."

"Maybe. She was up in years. I hope no harm came to her. Makes me wonder. She made quite a mark for herself in quilting circles, yet we didn't even know her name. I wish we had been more attentive to her and at least found out her name."

God's Pattern

We are never missing to God. We are all significant to Him; God knows our name. He redeems us and calls us His. God desires for us to look after one another. One of the blessings of fellowship in a healthy church is that there are others to check up on the old and lonely.

The Warmth of Hope

And hope does not disappoint us, because God has poured out his love into our hearts by the Holy Spirit, whom he has given us.

ROMANS 5:5 NIV

Wounded

But he was wounded for our transgressions, he was
bruised for our iniquities: the chastisement of our peace
was upon him; and with his stripes we are healed.
ISAIAH 53:5

*B*y the time Sandy reached Stan's bed in Walter
Reed Hospital, her emotions were exhausted from
the examples she had already seen of raw courage
and inspiring attitudes. Her jacket pocket was wet
from the soppy handkerchief she mopped her eyes
with between patients.

When Sandy laid the Ohio Star quilt she carried across the half-empty lap of a handsome blond
soldier, she whispered, "I'm sorry about your wound.
This quilt is to show we appreciate what you have
sacrificed for our country. We're grateful for your
service." She turned her head away, unable to watch
the tears well up in the soldier's eyes.

"Wait, lady." Stan grabbed her arm as she started
to move away. "It isn't losing my leg that gets to
me." Stan gave his face an impatient swipe with his
sleeve. "Your gift says someone knows what we did
for our country was important and thinks we made a

difference for good in the world." He cleared his throat. "Sure, it hurts plenty." He moved his stump. "I have phantom pain and wake up thinking my leg is still there. But the hard part is, I'm not sure everyone understands our enemy is real and determined."

Stan wheeled his chair closer. "These terrorists are dedicated to destroying our culture, to ending our way of life. If I gave a leg, and the others," he said gesturing around the hospital ward with his arm, "gave what they gave to expose the enemies' true goals, we've shown the nature of our enemy. We must defeat and stop the terrorist away from our own country."

> **Scrap Basket**
> Before women were given the right to vote, sometimes they expressed political opinions on their quilts.

He clutched the quilt with one hand as the other pounded the arm of his wheelchair. "I just wish more people were like you and could see it costs to have a great country like ours. My regret is that the way some people talk leaves our enemy feeling empowered to kill and destroy." He wiped his eyes with the red, white, and blue quilt. "I want others to understand the importance of what we're doing."

Sandy felt overwhelmed; then she leaned over and kissed his cheek, mingling her tears with his. "Thank you" was all she could whisper.

God's Pattern

Jesus died on the cross, supplying the sacrifice necessary to attain freedom from sin. In this sinful world, freedom from corrupt people and governments requires sacrifice. A society that does not understand the importance of standing against evil wherever it reigns will lose freedom on their own shores.

The Warmth of Hope

Be of good courage, and he shall strengthen your heart, all ye that hope in the LORD.

PSALM 31:24

Baby Complications

*All the days of the afflicted are evil: but he that
is of a merry heart hath a continual feast.*

PROVERBS 15:15

*R*ita walked in stocking feet toward the family room. At the door, she heard her daughter complaining.

"I'm sick of dusting." Cassie flung her feather duster down. "I want to play video games."

"Helping means Mamma's baby might stay alive this time." Kim swished her own feather duster across the pictures hung above the sofa.

"Maybe this baby will die like the other two babies." Cassie plopped down in a chair.

"Those were ectopic pregnancies." Kim flaunted her older-sister knowledge. "Mamma can't help it she has blood clots this time. A baby will be fun." Kim dusted her sister's head.

Cassie grabbed the duster. "A baby will be more work." She dusted Kim's shoes.

"Ready for quilt class?" The girls fell silent when Dad led Mom to the sofa, her shoes in his hand. "It's shoe time."

"Maybe I shouldn't go. I'm leaving so many jobs

to the girls," Rita said. "They'd rather be playing. I can always learn to quilt later."

"Home or out, you have to keep your feet up. Quilting class is the perfect plan. Your friend drives. You prop your legs up and learn to quilt while chatting with adults. The girls and I win the dust duel." Dad snatched Cassie's duster. *"En guarde!"* He assumed a fencing pose and jabbed Cassie in the ribs with the feathers. "We'll form a royal court when the baby arrives safely. The girls will be head princesses." He tickled both girls, then handed back the duster.

> ### Scrap Basket
> In early American history, women learned to quilt from family members; today, more women learn to quilt in classes.

"In the meantime, you're my Cinderella who needs shoes to go to the ball and learn to quilt." He knelt with Rita's shoes. "The girls are the cute little mice scurrying around to make Cinderella's house beautiful. I'm Prince Charming, and I'm determined to jam these shoes on your puffy little feet if I have to use soap to make them fit." Dad faked loud grunting noises as he shoved and shoved, while the girls collapsed laughing.

Rita giggled. "Oh, so romantic."

"The prince wants to play with the mice. Your coach is honking at the door. Quilting will give your mind something positive to think about."

Rita kissed her fair prince and took her quilt

bag from him. She stepped carefully off the front porch, knowing that his knack for role-playing kept everyone's hearts merry while waiting until her baby was born safely.

God's Pattern
The ability to apply generous doses of humor and dashes of fun to chores and worries lightens our hearts in the midst of dull routine or difficulties.

The Warmth of Hope
Why are you downcast, O my soul? Why so disturbed within me? Put your hope in God, for I will yet praise him, my Savior and my God.
PSALM 43:5 NIV

Stranger

The LORD is on my side; I will not fear:
what can man do unto me?
PSALM 118:6

"Nadia cries every time she's brought to my house," Dana said. "It doesn't matter what grandmotherly things I try to do. She's terror-stricken at my house."

Aretta, Nadia's paternal grandmother, shook her head. "She's the same way at my house. At first, I understood. It's a big event to uproot a two-year-old from a Russian orphanage, the only home she'd ever known."

"And it's a major adjustment to bring her to the United States, where no one speaks her language," Dana, the young immigrant's maternal grandmother, said. "But you'd think she would have adjusted and overcome such great fear by now. She's almost seven!"

Aretta grinned. "I must say I'm relieved to know she acts the same way at your home. I thought maybe I was the ogre grandma."

"No, I have monster status, too. I'm proud of your son and my daughter for adopting a Russian child, but I wish she'd adjusted better. It's hard on everyone seeing her so terrified. With this extreme separation anxiety, my daughter can't leave her to do anything without a problem. I keep praying for the child."

"When she's older, she'll realize coming here probably rescued her from a life of prostitution. The orphanages simply don't have the funds to feed all the children, which means many have to leave in their middle teens." Aretta shuddered. "With no way to earn a living, the girls sometimes resort to prostitution."

> **Scrap Basket**
> By 1880, American manufacturers produced large quantities and varieties of fabric, increasing the choices for beautiful quilts.

"I've been wondering if a security blanket would help." Dana picked up a quilt-pattern book. "A soft, comfy quilt."

"Good idea. What do you suggest?"

"We could make her a quilt to bring to our houses. It could be something that was just hers, that she could wrap up in anywhere." Dana showed Aretta a picture of one in her book. "Sunbonnet girl quilts are cute."

"Let's do it! Can't hurt, and it might help. Let's embroider a scripture verse about God's protection on each square. Maybe they will help Nadia turn to God for security."

Together the two grandmothers shopped for fabrics to coordinate the dresses and hats of the sunbonnet girls. The women divided up the fabric and began to appliqué the dolls on muslin squares.

"When you get yours done, give me a call. We can sew the squares together at my house and get caught up on all our talking while we quilt the blanket," Dana said. "We're blessed to be friends. Every in-law relationship isn't like ours. We can pray together for God to give Nadia stability."

God's Pattern
When Jesus becomes a personal reality in our situations, fear cannot stand in His presence. Our hope and faith in Him changes fear to trust in Him, enabling us to wait with patience.

The Warmth of Hope
But if we hope for that we see not, then do we with patience wait for it.

ROMANS 8:25

Prayer Ties

*Hear my prayer, O God; give
ear to the words of my mouth.*
PSALM 54:2

I hope people respond." Kay laid an indelible marker by the quilt that was spread over a big table near the front door of her quilt shop.

Stunned by reports of their coworker's serious illness, Sherrie's fellow employees at the quilt shop had set to work on what they did best when confronted with bad news: They made a quilt. Each of the store's employees sewed a block; now the finished quilt top, fastened to the batting and backing by safety pins, lay awaiting customers to tie it together.

"What's going on with Sherrie?" Lucy questioned after reading the sign asking customers to help complete the quilt—and pray.

"She has a chromosomal abnormality," Kay explained. "The treatments are dangerous, but she'll die without them. The store staff made the quilt to encourage her. We hope the customers she's helped will pray for her, too. When the quilt's tied, we'll give it to her to take to her tests and treatments and remind her she is covered by the prayers and love of our quilting community."

"I'm sorry to hear she's ill," Lucy said. "I love Sherrie. She's always smiling and gives the best advice about making quilts. What can I do?"

Kay handed her a needle from a pincushion full of others, already threaded with yarn. "Pick a corner of one of the squares, pull the yarn through all the layers, and tie a knot. Pray for Sherrie's healing while you do it. Then use the permanent pen and sign the square so she'll have a record of the customers who love her."

Kay wished Sherrie could be there to see the enthusiasm the customers had for her and hear their earnest prayers. More than once, damp spots from teary eyes formed on the fabric signatures. Sherrie's customers also promised to continue praying for her.

As each returned to the shop

> ### Scrap Basket
> Today, many quilts are made by busy women to express love and concern for others, often using fabric themes to reflect the recipient's hobbies or in colors to match their home's decor.

later, Kay had good news for them. Sherrie had phoned in, telling Kay that she carried her quilt to every test and treatment; then she hung it on the wall of her hospital room, where it reminded her she did not fight her battle alone. A battalion of prayer warriors joined her own prayers for God's healing touch. The quilt now hangs prominently in Sherrie's home, reminding her that her beloved customers sought her miraculous recovery.

God's Pattern

God hears our prayers. Our faith is strengthened when we know others are joining us in seeking God to heal and help our situation. Praying for others' needs is a gift of love. We won't know until we arrive in heaven the full impact of our prayers on earth.

The Warmth of Hope

Remember the word to Your servant,
in which You have made me hope.

PSALM 119:49 NASB

Disappointment

And we know that all things work together for
good to them that love God, to them who are
the called according to his purpose.
ROMANS 8:28

his is the most beautiful quilt our guild has ever worked on together," Fran commented, admiring the pastel colors.

"Ought to be! Never saw such gorgeous fabrics as the ones manufactured by the auction sponsor. Not to mention that our alternating star pattern is stunning, if I do say so myself," Beth added with pride.

"The best part will be the money it raises for the St. Jude's hospitals. It should bring several thousand dollars, don't you think?"

"I'm expecting the bidding to go very high. After all, we hand quilted it, and people like contributing to a worthy cause."

With a strong sense of satisfaction, the women boxed up their masterpiece and shipped it from Virginia to New Orleans for the auction, wondering what their efforts would earn.

Quilt seekers traveled from long distances to

attend the auction, which was scheduled for the morning of September 11, 2001. By nine o'clock, a good crowd had gathered in the New Orleans auction house to start the bidding on the quilts.

But the auction was short-lived. No sooner had the starting bid of two hundred dollars been made on the quilt from Virginia when someone rushed in and turned on the television in the corner of the room. The silent crowd stared as the news blared about a plane flying into the World Trade Center tower. Soon the stunned crowd watched another plane fly into the second tower. In the midst of the resulting confusion, people left the auction, scurrying to airports, train stations, and rent-a-car places. Uncertain what the event signified, the officials immediately stopped the auction, and the first bidder claimed the lovely alternating star quilt.

Scrap Basket
Every year, quilt auctions raise thousands of dollars that go to well-known and worthy charities.

Back in Virginia, the women who had invested vast amounts of time in the quilt were disappointed that their quilt failed to raise the money they had hoped for to donate to the hospitals, but it was a disappointment tempered by the same grief being felt nationwide. The quilt faded into the background.

A few months later, however, the fabric manufacturer, recognizing the quality of the quilt, used a picture of it in ads and flyers. The women felt the publicity validated their work and the anticipated, but not realized, worth of their quilt. Robbed of their goal for the work of their hands, the women concluded that God would turn their deferred hope into something good even if they never understood.

God's Pattern
God doesn't waste. Although the amount
of money the quilt raised for an esteemed
hospital was a disappointment, the women
had enjoyed creating a lovely object and were
glad the sponsor published pictures of their
finished project. As a result, others could copy
their design and create something lovely for
themselves. If we ask Him, God will take our
disappointments and turn them into something
that blesses others and us. Our role is to trust
that blessings will finally come. The end result
may become sweeter than our original hopes.

The Warmth of Hope
Hope deferred maketh the heart sick: but when
the desire cometh, it is a tree of life.
PROVERBS 13:12

Taggie Quilts

Shout for joy, O heavens; rejoice, O earth; burst into song, O mountains! For the LORD comforts his people and will have compassion on his afflicted ones.
ISAIAH 49:13 NIV

Val, the hospital volunteer, laughed. "Look at Butch. He has a beautiful quilt of colorful animals, and what does he focus on? The tag."

"He likes the tag's silky feeling," Maribeth, Butch's mother said. Two-year-old Butch kept rubbing the tag, his eyelids drooping. Maribeth lowered her voice. "I don't understand the psychology, but he settles down and goes to sleep when he finds the tag on his quilt and strokes it. I'm grateful when he can sleep in spite of his pain. That tag is worth a purse of gold to me. It's hard watching your child suffer."

Val put her arm around Maribeth's shoulders and stood, watching as Butch drifted off to sleep. "That gives me an idea," she said.

Several months later, Val brought a basket of small quilts to give the children on the hospital's pediatric floor. Wide chunks of satin ribbon were sewn at intervals around all the edges of each quilt. By bedtime, her work was rewarded. Children up and down the unit fell asleep with their fingers stroking the satin finish of the ribbons on their quilts.

Val peeked into room after room. Parents, faces worn with worry, smiled back at her and whispered their thanks for the "Taggie" quilt with

> ### Scrap Basket
> Crazy quilts have enjoyed several periods of popularity. When silk was hard to obtain, women sometimes used the lining of men's hats.

its marvelous comforting effect. The satin texture soothed restless patients to sleep.

A tradition began. Val enlisted others to make and pass out the much-coveted Taggie quilts on the children's floor, where small symbols of security were gratefully grasped.

God's Pattern

God desires to comfort us in our every
need. He sent the Holy Spirit to surround
us with comfort when we experience sickness
or walk through the valley of death. John 14:16
says, "And I will pray the Father, and he
shall give you another Comforter, that he
may abide with you for ever"; God's comfort
is as close as our whisper for help.

The Warmth of Hope

We might have a strong consolation, who have
fled for refuge to lay hold upon the hope set
before us: Which hope we have as an anchor
of the soul, both sure and stedfast.

HEBREWS 6:18–19

Border Exchange

Better is the end of a thing than the beginning
thereof: and the patient in spirit is better
than the proud in spirit.
ECCLESIASTES 7:8

I can't believe it," Wilma sputtered when her quilt was returned to her after it had made the rounds of seven guild members for the guild's first border exchange.

"A common reaction whenever guilds are brave enough to hold a border exchange." Tina patted her hand.

"But I wrote a note explaining I wanted the quilt to be very traditional. All the fabric I enclosed from the center block was very traditional. Not to mention, the Ohio Star center block I made is tradition in itself." Wilma restrained herself from wailing.

"Traditional it's not, at least not since your esteemed guild members added their various borders around the four sides." A giggle escaped from Tina. "Just look. This border has origami flowers on it."

"And beads, of all things, are sewn all over this border." Wilma's chagrin turned into a grin.

Tina laughed. "And what is it about traditional that you don't understand when you use contemporary batik fabric?"

"I have to admit the green and purple blend of colors is pretty. You know that is the color scheme of my best friend's bedroom. The most handmade thing she makes is a grocery list. I'll bet she'd love this quilt for her birthday."

And she did. "My friend was absolutely thrilled with the quilt," Wilma reported to Tina after she had given the quilt away. "You know it really was pretty. It just wasn't what I had visualized. But it made a lovely gift."

"A blessing in disguise, even if it didn't turn out like you wanted," Tina said.

"But I'll never take part in a border exchange again."

Tina grinned. "Blessing or no, very few ever do repeat that kind of exchange again."

God's Pattern

God's kingdom is big enough to encompass
people of every kind of taste and talent. Variety
is a blessing in the hand of God, because what
reaches one person and brings them revelation
about God may be very different from what
touches the heart of the next person.

The Warmth of Hope

"But now, Lord, what do I look for?
My hope is in you."

PSALM 39:7 NIV

We Won't Forget

*And he said unto them, Go ye into all the world,
and preach the gospel to every creature.*
MARK 16:15

The air tingled with the girls' excitement. "Quiet," Mrs. Lillian requested.

"I used the red marker to trace my hand." Polly pointed to her handprint.

"Mine's blue." Tenesha placed her hand on top of her print.

"Everybody, sit down and listen." Mrs. Lillian's patience was frayed from sitting up late the night before, sewing together all the squares with handprints from three Sunday school classes. She held up the finished quilt top full of handprints. "Tonight we're going to tie the three layers of our quilt together. Since the going-away party for the Collier family is after church tomorrow, we have to finish it tonight."

Mrs. Lillian managed to get the eager group threading needles, sewing through the layers, and tying knots; but she didn't try to stop the loud chatter.

"Is it cold in Mongolia?"

"The Colliers will live in the mountain region, which can be very cold," Mrs. Lillian answered.

"How will all three Collier girls fit under one quilt?"

"In Mongolia, people raise lots of sheep. They'll have wool blankets, too. Our quilt will help them remember us and to remember we are praying for them as they adjust to living in a new and strange place."

Tenesha's lip trembled. "I'd cry if I had to go far away around the world. Cathy's my very best friend. Maybe I'll never see her again."

> **Scrap Basket**
> Quilts often accompanied pioneers. The first Caucasian woman to climb Pike's Peak in Colorado carried a quilt in her pack.

"Now, girls. The family is going to Mongolia to tell boys and girls who live there about Jesus. We are very proud of them. We'll see them every other year when they come back to the United States for visits. They'll tell us interesting stories about their adventures in Mongolia and the girls they meet.

"I'm still going to cry at the party," Polly said.

Both of the little girls were right. There were lots of tears, but the special quilt gift brought smiles, too, especially from the Collier girls, Cathy, Chloe, and Connie.

"We outlined our hands and wrote our names so you won't forget us," Tenesha explained.

Cathy, the oldest, spoke for her sisters. "We won't forget. We'll put our hands on the handprints, and we'll feel like we're holding hands with our friends back home."

God's Pattern
Ever since Jesus rose from the dead,
missionaries have traveled to introduce people
in other countries to the gospel message.
Obeying God's instructions to leave our
familiar lifestyle and become missionaries
requires sacrifice. We support our missionaries
with our prayers, financial support, and
encouraging correspondence from home.

The Warmth of Hope
For thou art my hope, O Lord God:
thou art my trust from my youth.

PSALM 71:5

I Believe

And when he was come into the house, the blind men came to him: and Jesus saith unto them, Believe ye that I am able to do this? They said unto him, Yea, Lord.
MATTHEW 9:28

The news kept getting worse. Kara and her husband, Warren, held hands as they listened to the grim diagnosis and drastic surgical steps the doctor proposed. "I am a child of the most high God," Kara whispered suddenly, and Warren gripped her hand tighter. Her characteristic proclamation of faith accompanied her tears. She wiped them from her cheeks, even her neck. The neck the doctor's proposed surgery would mangle. Her hands slid over her smooth skin. *I'll never be the same.*

"I believe God," Kara sang, almost defiantly, on the drive home. She and Warren quoted Bible verses to bolster their faith that God was with them in this nightmare. The tests ordered to investigate a lump in Kara's throat would be the beginning of a long ordeal, but they were confident God would see them through.

Abruptly Kara sat up straighter in the car, and

Warren could sense another declaration coming.

"I'm going to make a quilt."

Warren smiled. *How like Kara.* Making a quilt was her response to everything.

"It'll be my faith quilt," Kara explained as they entered their home. She headed straight for her sewing room and began sorting through her fabric stash. "It'll be a witness to God's love and goodness to everyone involved in the long hospital stay and rehabilitation time." Spreading a number of pieces out on her cutting board, she snipped out blue and white squares, brainstorming aloud about what she would write on the white pieces. "I am the Lord who heals you," joined other words that proclaimed her faith.

The quilt progressed as the test results were received and the date of surgery planned. Her fingers flew, right up to the day she went in, while her church family gathered, praying fervently as she faced the potentially disfiguring surgery for cancer.

Kara awoke slowly, barely aware of the light in the dim room. The first face she saw was her husband's, and his voice was a bare whisper.

"Dr. Adams didn't cut as much as he planned." Warren's words swam through postsurgical pain and anesthesia haze, but she smiled; and her eyes wandered to her quilt, which was draped over a chair next to her bed. Throughout her hospital stay, the quilt stimulated conversations with each member of the staff who saw her. Contrary to predictions, she could talk a little bit when pointing to her quilt words.

Kara's hospital room soon resounded with rejoicing over the lab results. Her lump wasn't cancer. "God performed a miracle while I was on the operating table," she declared to everyone who would listen.

> *Scrap Basket*
> Women for generations have found the creative process of quilting brings comfort in trying circumstances.

Long months of therapy brought more miracles of head movement, most of them defying the predictions of her medical team.

"Want to take a break?" her therapist asked regularly.

"No. I want to move my head normally." Swiping at therapy-induced tears, Kara persisted.

"I wanted everyone to rejoice in the goodness of God," Kara told her guests at the party she later held for those who had stood with her, believing God for His mercy toward her. Her "ordeal" had come full circle, and Kara rejoiced as each guest signed the quilt, her tangible reminder of a strong, miraculous faith.

God's Pattern

The Bible is full of God's promises to heal,
along with other promises to bless His people.
Reading and memorizing His promises builds
our faith, helping us walk through difficult
times when our faith would fail. We need one
another's faith in times of trouble.

The Warmth of Hope

Let Israel hope in the LORD
from henceforth and for ever.

PSALM 131:3